Intelligent Shepherding
The Model of Spiritual Counseling for

DELIVERANCE

MARCOS DE SOUZA BORGES
(COTY)

BALBOA
PRESS

A DIVISION OF HAY HOUSE

Balboa Press books may be ordered through booksellers or by contacting:

Balboa Press
A Division of Hay House
1663 Liberty Drive
Bloomington, IN 47403
www.balboapress.com
1 (877) 407-4847

Print information available on the last page.

ISBN: 978-1-5043-8826-9 (sc)
ISBN: 978-1-5043-8828-3 (hc)
ISBN: 978-1-5043-8827-6 (e)

Library of Congress Control Number: 2017916783

Balboa Press rev. date: 11/20/2017

Table of Contents

Part I

Basic Concepts

1

INTRODUCTION

There is a "new tolerance" that has been spawned in our modern society that is based on both an inversion and an aversion to biblical values; it has produced a "new generation" that is very differentiated. We face the worst kind of spiritual attack that the church could suffer, a moral permissiveness that is associated with technological advancement and it has engendered a culture that is increasingly global and anti-Christian. This has directly affected the family makeup and the health of the church.

The actual situation of the church is always a reflection of what is happening in the family. Starting from the premise that the family is the cell of society, what we have today is a gigantic social cancer. "The family is terminal," declares the French psychoanalyst Charles Melman in a recent article in Veja magazine. He says: "We have witnessed an event that might not have precedent in history, the dissolution of the family group. For the first time the institution of the family is disappearing, and the consequences are unpredictable."

Western (American) society has best defined and modeled the family institution. The result has been that it became immeasurably stronger than any that has existed before it. However, since the 60's a growing backlash has been occurring. Perhaps a brief historical overview of the dysfunctionalization of the family that has been spreading worldwide is in order:

— It began with the decriminalization of adultery and the famous no fault divorce in the U.S. during the decades of the 60's and 70's.

— It was followed by the culture of non-marriage (free sex, drugs and rock 'n roll). This culture has spread so widely that currently, in addition to heterosexuals not wanting to marry, homosexuals are fighting for the right to marry.

— Consequently, an epidemic of pregnant adolescents and juvenile parents is multiplying in a generational cycle that has reduced parenthood to an average age of 15.

— This has spawned the sinister, gigantic, abortion industry, where millions of children have been murdered by the very people who should most accept, protect and love them. It is difficult to assess the imbalance of injustice that has spiritually accumulated with so much bloodshed.

— All this has produced an exponential increase of psychoemotional disorders. Research shows that in thirty years the percentage of the American population with depressive disorders has risen from 3% to 30%.

— The loss of existential ties has exorbitantly elevated the indexes of abuse and violence. Single mothers and fathers are marginalized and children have been made vulnerable, producing miserable families. This is the recipe for a proliferation of pedophilia, child prostitution, pornography and all forms of violence and sexual perversion.

This platform of familial bankruptcy gives birth to and nurtures a legacy of misery and violence. It produces a scenario of urban warfare that spreads panic, especially in large cities. Essentially, this social pathology based on violence and crime is simply a side effect of the death of the family — the tragic reaction of a generation that has been deprived of existential relationships and therefore suffers every variation of perverted, criminal and amoral behavior.

— We have created confusion between correction and violence, i.e., there has been so much abuse that the government directly interferes in how parents educate their children. We have a delinquent generation that is growing up without correction and increasingly has less respect for parents or any type of authority.

A zealous mother in a church where I ministered was being threatened with losing custody of her son. The reason was that she was punishing him by spanking him using a switch she would take from an outside bush. After explaining biblically to the policeman who came to her door why she was correcting her son in this manner, she asked him: "Do you know why I'm using this switch to correct my son when it is necessary?" He responded: "Why?" She said: "Do you see that baton hanging on your belt?" "Yes," he replied. "If I don't correct my son with a switch, it won't be long before it will be YOU who will be hitting him with your baton!"

— And finally, we have the homosexual dictatorship. This dictatorship is established by a lack of discernment between acceptance and approval. Acceptance is unconditional, linked to the intrinsic value of humans; however, approval is conditional and depends on character, i.e., choices. To accept someone regardless of their choices is a matter of civility; to be obligated to approve a conduct that attacks your values is abuse. Despite accepting such a person, those who do not approve homosexual conduct are ostensibly marginalized and discriminated against, all in the name of prejudice. With this, the process of social anarchy seems to hit the bottom of the barrel.

Studying the fall and destruction of great empires and societies that have marked human history (the Assyrians, Babylonians, Romans, Incas, etc.) it is clear that there are common aspects with what we are seeing today:

- **Moral relativity**. Society whose fundamentals are profoundly threatened by the trivialization of sin and the legalization of wickedness.
- **Perversion and animalization of sex**. Hedonistic pleasure at the expense of marriage, pleasure for pleasure's sake, where relationships are disposable.
- **Loss of family ties**. When a critical mass of society finds itself disconnected from essential relationships and does not know who is the father, mother, husband, wife, child, etc.
- **Explicit occultism**. A growing and explicit involvement with satanic rituals. The era of witches, wizards and vampires.

This has been the challenging backdrop of Western society. If we do not respond as the church, certainly we will be doomed to inevitable destruction.

The role of the church

We need to adjust pastorally to interact with the whole arena of these challenges or, to the contrary, even though the harvest may be great, the fruits will be quickly lost. There are many who try to stay in church even though they are spiritually sick but end up relinquishing their faith and dying spiritually. And this is when they have not experienced spiritual abuse that has traumatized them even further, accelerating the losses. Worse yet is that all of this has been highly advantageous to a gospel that is increasingly humanistic, permissive and decentralized from the glory of God.

Today, the ministerial demand is to close the doors of the church. This has given innumerous pastors great difficulty. This ministerial failing has produced an absurd population of more than 40 million de-churched in Brazil.[1] This is a population that is equivalent to the entire Brazilian evangelical population! As many who are now currently in church have now fallen away from church and have become disillusioned with it. The result: a post-Christian generation; a people who are being transformed into the worst people in society.

This leads us to a sad conclusion about the growth of evangelicals: the majority of the growth is of poor quality and actually results in huge losses to the church. This ecclesiastical paradigm does not prioritize the health and quality of growth and needs to be confronted.

The qualification process of growth demands that we think not only in transformation, i.e., a change of form, but in transfoundation, a change in fundamentals, values and cultures in relation to this new generation that is coming into our churches, a process which is only possible by the wisdom of the cross.

Obviously, a great deal of effort on the part of pastors is necessary to mature a new convert and it is even more difficult to create

---

[1] In the U.S., every year, 2.7 million church members fall into inactivity. This translates into the realization that people are leaving the church. From our research, we have found that they are leaving as hurting and wounded victims—of some kind of abuse, disillusionment, or just plain neglect! (http://www.intothyword. org/articles_view.asp?articleid=36557) Francis A. Schaeffer Institute of Church Leadership Development (FASICLD).

Most of the statistics tell us that nearly 50% of Americans have no church home. In the 1980s, membership in the church had dropped almost 10%; then, in the 1990s, it worsened by another 12% drop—some denominations are reporting a 40% drop in their membership. And now, over half way through the first decade of the 21st century, we are seeing the figures drop even more!

Recent studies and surveys by sociologists and political scientists that utilize more complex definitional parameters have estimated the number of evangelicals in the U. S. at about 25-30% of the population, or roughly between 70 and 80 million people. (http://isae.wheaton.edu/defining-evangelicalism/how-many-evangelicals-are-there).

a disciple; the huge investment required to produce an ideal, trusted leader dwarfs both. Without laying solid groundwork in discipleship, the process of sanctification stagnates and, in more cases than not, is aborted before it even begins.

The majority of pastors can describe their ministry as an exhausting routine of "putting out fires" and "pastoral crises" on the part of their members and disciples. They are not pastoring people, they are pastoring their crises; they are pastoral firemen. The basics are not being addressed. Besides being exhausting, this reality does not create viable solutions that enable stable growth. Pastoral effort is often merely the equivalent of applying a band-aid and the crisis cycle continues unabated. The church becomes increasing shallow and dull.

Responding to the appeal of countless leaders, pastors, missionaries and intercessors who aspire to efficient and intelligent pastoral training, the transfoundational approach aims to educate the body of Christ with biblical principles and values; it invests in the health of the church, especially in her qualitative growth, and redeems the values of the priestly-pastoral role in a profound and contextualized manner while addressing the emerging needs of this generation.

This model of deliverance counseling establishes an approach centered on principles and demystifies the concepts of deliverance, healing, authority and pastoral maturity. It enables those who feel the responsibility to help others to have a firm base in counseling, deliverance, re-education of character and identity, generational restoration, reconciliation, etc. The objective is to dynamically promote the sanctification of the church from a fundamental and practical point of view.

BASIC INSIGHTS

Before going into the diagram of the counseling model of deliverance, it is important to lay some groundwork about the basic concepts:

1. EXPELLING DEMONS VS. DELIVERANCE

The word "deliverance" in evangelical culture has historically been used exclusively for the expulsion of demons. However, in our model of spiritual counseling, it is important that we make a distinction between "expelling demons" and "deliverance." This is a distinction that is quite clear in Jesus' ministry. In some of the narratives Jesus directly casts out demons, but in others the individual's deliverance comes without any demon being excised.

The expelling of demons is normally associated with the process of evangelization. The evangelistic ministry is almost always accompanied by two gifts: healing the sick and expelling demons. When there is a demonic manifestation during a presentation of the gospel, the demon is expelled so the person is free to consider accepting Jesus. The objective is to clear the path for the person to make an objective decision about salvation. Once he has accepted Jesus, is he totally free and has all of his past been completely resolved? Of course not! It will be necessary to address the reasons that the demonic exploitation was present to begin with.

Truthfully, demons are merely spiritual parasites that feed off of human injustices. They are an indirect consequence of spiritual warfare. Imagine a location where trash is accumulating. Obviously there will be many flies and other vermin like cockroaches and rats attracted to the trash. How do you combat these parasites? It does not matter how much you shoo away the flies, stomp on the cockroaches or kill the rats, they will multiply faster than you can eliminate them and will end up returning, continuously infesting the environment.

We call this the "shoo fly" method of ministry when we insist on irresponsibly expelling someone's demons. However, if instead of swatting mosquitoes and squashing cockroaches, you decide to eliminate the garbage and disinfect the environment, you will automatically eliminate the parasites and they will not return. This is deliverance. True deliverance means that you are responsibly—and personally—dealing with the generational and territorial garbage of the soul. We will explain later that the deliverance of the soul is directly related to the conversion process and goes further than the concept of the new birth.

There is no value in becoming a specialist in parasites, learning their hierarchy or the different types of flies, rats, etc., that exist In deliverance the emphasis needs to be on the garbage. When you eliminate the trash the parasites will leave with it!

The essence of deliverance is sanctification. The presence of demons and curses is symptomatic and secondary. It is necessary to identify and responsibly deal with the causes of spiritual problems:

memories wounded by guilt; shame; abuse and hidden trauma; strong, sinful ties; hidden sins; iniquities, generational and territorial wounds that exert a pervasive influence; broken relationships; chronic enmities; marital trauma; broken alliances, family crises, etc.

2. DEMYSTIFYING CURSES

When we begin to talk about curses people typically react negatively. Some express an aversion to the topic; others classify it as heresy and become theologically indignant. There really is much "strange fire" and disequilibrium associated with it, as much in teaching as in the practice of dealing with it. The evangelical world is full of superstitions. Every faith that does not have a biblical base is superstitious and mystical. We need to demystify this:

a. The world "curse" is a biblical word.

First, the word "curse" does not have its origins in the occult, rather, it is a biblical word that occurs more than 200 times in the Bible. As such, it is something that should not be despised. As much as it is stigmatized, as much as we dislike it, as much as it does not sit well with us and as much as we see it as a deplorable concept, "curse" is a biblical word that merits the effort necessary to understand it.

There are several words in the Bible that are translated as "curse." Basically all of them can be summarized by one of three meanings:

- A punishment coming from the breach of a commandment, a covenant with God, or breaking a promise or oath. The word in the Old Testament is *alah*; in the New Testament the word is *anathema*, which also signifies that which is prohibited under the penalty of punishment or destruction.
- A situation where something or someone is bound (as with a spell), hemmed in with obstacles, rendered powerless to resist. It is exactly the opposite condition of the blessing of God. The Hebrew word *arar* references an actual curse or one who has been cursed.
- A curse arising from speaking evil, swearing, defaming, cursing, wishing harm. In the Old Testament the words are *qalal*,

qabab, *naqab* and *za'am* and they basically have the same meaning. In the New Testament there are the words *kataraomai*, *kakologeo* and *raca* (insult). This is a spoken curse and represents an open, public expression of emotional hostility against one's enemy. Jesus warned us about it saying: *"Curse no one."* He also said we should bless those who curse us in this manner.

b. Almost every time the word "curse" occurs in the Bible, it appears in the context of the people of the covenant and not unbelievers or the wicked.

Perhaps this surprises you. It is natural to conclude that the wicked or unbelieving will be in a spiritually unfavorable condition. A curse does not seem to be appropriate way to characterize the life of a believer. However, in the Bible, the word is almost always associated with the people of the covenant, the people who should be the guardians of the divine precepts and commands. The blessings we enjoy because of the Bible are not a permanent inheritance. Our choices determine whether or not we remain secure in them.

Every alliance, commandment, law or principle carries a curse with it. You have the option of obeying counsel; not so with an alliance, commandment, law or principle. They carry consequences:

> *"But if you refuse to listen to the Lord your God and do not obey all the commands and decrees I am giving you today, all these curses will come and overwhelm you"* (Dt 28:15).

Reading these words you have to remember that God was not referring to the wicked, but to his own people. It illustrates the responsibility implicit in an alliance with Him. The possibility of curse comes with the alliance. You might think that this is an Old Testament issue; however, the writer of Hebrews shows to what degree it is found in the New Testament: *"For it is impossible to bring back to repentance those who were once enlightened—those who have experienced the good things of heaven and shared in the Holy Spirit, who have tasted the goodness of the word of God and the power of the age to come—and who then turn away from God. It is impossible to bring such people back to repentance; by rejecting the Son of God, they themselves are nailing him to the cross once again and holding him up to public shame" (Hb 6:4-6).*

This text has a very specific context that should not be generalized frivolously. It presents a specific manner to deal with a significant portion of the Jewish church that was falling away from Christianity into Jewish legalism. The point is that the New Testament reinforces the covenant responsibility implicit on the part of a believer.

c. The principal role of a curse is to denounce either aggregated, corporate, spiritual disorders or accumulated personal, generational or territorial disorders.

A curse provides a fundamental service. Despite being clothed with negative connotations, a curse in essence is a blessing. This seems to be a paradox. Our body has a series of warning mechanisms (such as pain, fever, vomiting, etc.) that alert us to more serious issues that are about to occur. Are these mechanisms good or bad? Just because something is classified as good does not mean that it will be pleasant. Pain is obviously not pleasant, but it plays an important role. When you have pain, it simply indicates that there is a problem exactly at that location. The pain alerts us that we need to treat the problem. If it were not for the pain, the problem could evolve to the point that it would put our life at risk. The worst and more dangerous disorders or diseases are the silent ones that can kill us without giving the slightest warning.

Thinking in this manner, pain is good, despite it being unpleasant. It forces us into a process of restoration (correction and education) that will lead us back to health. In light of this, it becomes easier to see a curse as a divine mechanism. A curse (which can come in the form of persecution, sickness, collapses, demonic attacks, etc.) denounces the existence of spiritual problems which we are not taking steps to resolve.

Even though the divine motive behind a curse is to alert, correct and save us, there does exist the possibility that it can destroy us. It can painfully lead us down the return path to a relationship with God; this relationship gives our life its eternal meaning. This produces obedience, maturity and genuine priesthood. A curse, as incredible as it seems, is a blessing! For this reason, wanting to "break a curse" without dealing directly with the inherent spirit problems is nothing more than pure ignorance!

d. The essence of a curse is punishment.

The verb punish comes from Latin and literally means to purify by suffering. The objective of a curse, as incredible as it may seem, is to correct our path. God corrects the child He loves (Hb 12:7). We have a tendency to think that a curse is something negative that obligatorily repeats itself in our lives like karma. However, in the Bible, the word does not have a fatalistic connotation; to the contrary, a curse is a message to help us discern our spiritual problems so we can personally and sacerdotally repair them.

Laws govern every aspect of the universe. When one disobeys a law they will suffer the respective consequences. A person can intentionally or accidentally put their hand in a fire, but in either case they will be burned. God is not cursing them. They are simply suffering the consequence of not respecting the limits established by a law.

Spiritually, things function in the same manner, though with different agents. Divine law has already sentenced Satan and his demons. Because of human injustice, these agents now play the role of accusing, afflicting, harassing, stealing, killing...

A moral realm requires a system of trial, correction and punishment. Every court of law is based on the Bible; the Bible defines the principal elements of a court: the judge, the defendant, the defense counsel and the accused. Humans are inherently accountable. The book of Job shows how God gave the devil permission to monitor the earth and appear before His tribunal, in a capacity obviously limited by His justice, tolerance and kindness.

The Bible does not present the concept of atonement where punishment is dispensed with exactness. God's laws are reasonable. His commandments are safeguards for everyone, not merely negative prohibitions. When divine law prohibits theft it safeguards the right to property. For law to have value, it is necessary to have a punishment for those who break it. The purpose of a sanction is to prevent the act from being repeated; hence, the most important aspect of law is to deter future disobedience. It is clear that God's laws are good and fair for everyone, without exception. Consequently, He expects our obedience. Therefore there will always be punishment (curse) for violators.

To say that curses do not exist is to affirm that sin has no consequence. This is ridiculous. Some say that they can freely sin because

God has already forgiven them in Christ. While this may be true, this sort of sophistry ignores the consequences that will certainly visit them and/or remain permanently in their life, their marriage, with their children, etc. Sowing is a choice, harvesting is an obligation.

e. A curse is from God, not the devil.

Perhaps this also surprises you, but the one who strikes the earth with curses is God, not the devil. Through the prophet Malachi God affirms that He is the primary architect behind curses: *"His preaching will turn the hearts of fathers to their children, and the hearts of children to their fathers. Otherwise I will come and strike the land with a curse" (Ml 4:6)*. The Bible presents God as the supreme and perfect ruler of the universe. He claims all responsibility regarding good and evil: *"I create the light and make the darkness. I send good times and bad times. I, the Lord, am the one who does these things" (Is 45:7)*.

The word "create" here is not *"bará"* (create from nothing), but *"yatsar,"* to create in virtue of disobedience, wickedness, injustice or rebellion that is carried out systematically. Although often the wickedness is proposed and executed by Satan, it is authorized from the throne of God, which is founded on justice, judgment, truth and mercy (Ps 89:14).

This type of evil is created (by God) in virtue of another evil practiced (by man) in order to correct the situation. This is well exemplified in Ahab's death (2 Ch 18:18-22), one of the wickedest kings Israel ever had. Originally God did not create "evil" but merely the "possibility to know evil:" *"The Lord God made all sorts of trees grow up from the ground... and the tree of the knowledge of good and evil" (Gn 2:9)*.

There is not a dispute between God and the devil over power. This is undisputed. The destiny of everyone who chooses wickedness is already sealed. This is not the question. Demons are peripherals, parasites. The Bible does not present Satan as the protagonist of human history. On the contrary, he appears little in the Bible and always peripherally, as Peter says: *"Watch out for your great enemy, the devil. He prowls around like a roaring lion, looking for someone to devour" (1 Pe 5:8)*. He simply takes advantage of human disobedience.

Considering the emphasis we should give to demonic action, John Dawson in his book[1] *Healing America's Wounds*, gives a description that fits very well here:

> In Deuteronomy 28 we have a long list of curses that come as a consequence of disobeying the alliance established with God. This is not an angry Creator losing control of Himself and creating a ruckus.
>
> Deuteronomy 28 also is not a warning about some weakness of God's character. This same celestial Father was revealed in Jesus. The trial of Jesus in Gethsemane and the cross held greater temptation to become vengeful than has been experienced by anyone in the universe, but He maintained His self-control. It is no wonder that we can trust Him.
>
> In a sense, a curse can be seen as the absence of the need for God. Many understand that God is holy and that sin causes the withdrawal of His revealed presence, but our tendency is to think that things simply continue as they are when the truth is that the wages of sin is death. Consequences come. Look again at Deuteronomy 28. It is a litany of death.
>
> The revealed presence of God is not extra-optional. The worse thing that can be written about your life, your church, your city or your nation is Ichabod – *"The glory has departed" (1 Sm 4:21).* God does not abdicate one square foot of His government on this planet. His persistent grace continues. *"Where sin increased, grace abounded all the more" (Rm 5:20).* Yet His revealed presence remains hidden: *"You have hidden yourself in a cloud so our prayers cannot reach you" (Lm 3:44).*
>
> Worse than the presence of the enemy is the curse that results when the Lord turns His face away from us. This was what happened to Israel at Ai because of the sin of Achan: *"That is why the Israelites are running from their enemies in defeat. For now Israel itself has been set apart for destruction. I will not remain with you any longer" (Js 7:12).*

---

[1] John Dawson, *"Healing America's Wounds"*.

Therefore, our primary objective in intercession and deliverance is not the removal of the enemy but the return of the glory and the restoration of God's necessary favor. It is not a testimony of the presence of a strong demon when we find a spiritual stronghold, but rather the absence of the glory of God. In the same manner that nature abhors a vacuum, so it is in the spiritual realms when the glory departs, the demons arrive.

Think about the days of Nehemiah. His task was to rebuild Jerusalem. One of the priorities was to repair the gates, i.e., the legitimate entry ways and the place of authority and decision-making. But what about the holes in the walls?

It was there that the enemy attacked with a spirit of accusation and confusion. *"But when Sanballat and Tobiah and the Arabs, Ammonites, and Ashdodites heard that the work was going ahead and that the gaps in the wall of Jerusalem were being repaired, they were furious. They all made plans to come and fight against Jerusalem and throw us into confusion" (Ne 4:7, 8).*

What would you have done? If I had been in Nehemiah's place I would have probably ordered an immediate military assault against this nuisance. But Nehemiah was wiser. His priority was the construction of the wall. While each worker had to wear his sword, he also had to continue working. Nehemiah did not permit the enemy's presence to distract him from his primary task. *"I am engaged in a great work, so I can't come. Why should I stop working to come and meet with you?" (Ne 6:3).*

Are these the priorities of intercessors today? Are we hunting the enemy or repairing the wall? Of course we have the authority to remove the demons, but is that our primary task?

f. A curse is a generational disconnection.

Returning to Malachi 4:6, this becomes very clear. This biblical information is essential. He declares that if parents do not look after their children, the children will not look up to their parents. When the injustices, abandonment, immorality, abuse, etc., of the parents matches up to the rebellion and disrespect of the children (i.e., there is a disconnection between the generations), a curse installs itself through misfortunes and spiritual attacks, guaranteeing that the failure of the parents will repeat in the reality of the children.

This is the generational breach: parents provoke their children to anger and the children do not listen to their parents. They are spiritually set adrift by bitterness and rebellion. This was the story of Cain, Esau, Absalom and many of us. This breaking of relationship between parents and children distorts one's identity, damages their emotional capacity to establish relationships and demonizes their inheritance of posterity, causing the children to continue to repeat the mistakes of their parents. These family legacies should not be interpreted fatalistically. They are realities that can and should be sacerdotally redeemed. *"Together as one body, Christ reconciled both groups to God by means of his death on the cross, and our hostility toward each other was put to death"* (Ep 2:16).

Reconciliation is the way to address curses: between parents and children, husband and wife, leader and follower, between races, nations, etc. You cannot "break" a curse in the name of Jesus independently of undoing the imbalance of injustice and accumulated bitterness of relationships. It is not until someone decides personally or intercessorially to place themselves in the generational gap, confessing and forgiving generational iniquities, redeeming the sin of parents and the dishonor of children, reconciling hearts, healing wounds, that curses can begin to be resolved.

You should not use the name of Jesus as a lucky charm nor use the new birth as the only argument against curses. It does not work that way biblically. The principal biblical condition to crucify curses is based on reconciliation.

3. NEW BIRTH VS. SOUL CONVERSION

For the majority of believers these two concepts mean the same thing. Confusing them can create wrong theological paradigms and frustrating results.

The Bible says it is necessary to be born again. While it is logical to state that the new birth covers the initial aspect of the soul's conversion, it is only the beginning. The new birth addresses the human spirit. The Spirit of God recreates the human spirit and begins to inhabit it. This is what we call salvation. It is an instantaneous event; it is a new birth of the human spirit; it is a regeneration of spiritual life. Just believe in the redemptive work of Jesus and make the decision to follow him. Such faith comes supernaturally from repentance initiated by the preaching of the message of the Gospel. It is easy to be born again.

But there is another word: CONVERT. It is a word with a different meaning. Conversion is a continuous process of the regeneration of the soul. This takes time and has a price. It demands a change of direction, values and paradigms in several aspects, synchronizing our thoughts with the thoughts of God and affects all our behavior and relationships.

Therefore, to be born again is an instant regeneration of the spirit while conversion is the persevering process of deliverance and regeneration of the soul. Salvation is free, but becoming a disciple will cost you everything.

You can be saved and not converted. Why? Because conversion takes place in the soul. Salvation takes place in the spirit. You can be saved, have a spirit enlivened by the presence of God, be a new creature in Christ and still not be converted in your soul in many areas of your life.

What is your soul? You are a triune being: a body, a soul and a spirit (1 Th 5:23). Your spirit is the part of your being where you experience the conscience, communion and intuition of God. You soul is basically your mind, your will and your emotions. Your body is your house. Jesus can save your spirit in an instant, but your soul requires a long time to be converted.

Nothing is more dangerous than a saved human who has not been converted. You know that you are born again but sill think with the old mind, your old habits still dominate you, some attitudes have not changed, some wrong ways of thinking still continue the same. Negative convictions are still present. Evil thoughts still frequent your mind and attempt to strangle the voice of the conscience. Corruption, bitterness, envy and hate still continue to exist. You continue to fight against some uncontrolled desires. But you are saved. You do not know how long the Holy Spirit will struggle with your flesh, but until then, you are still saved.

A decontextualized teaching

> *"He died for everyone so that those who receive his new life will no longer live for themselves. Instead, they will live for Christ, who died and was raised for them. So we have stopped evaluating others from a human point of view... This means that anyone who belongs to Christ has become a new person. The old life is gone; a new life has begun!" (2 Co 5:15-17).*

I want to touch on a very delicate issue that is theologically troubling. I know that it is not easy to change a doctrinal point of view, especially given that even I had to do it and is was a difficult experience.

Truthfully, it would be very disingenuous to create a doctrine concerning curses based on verse 17 of this text by saying that the old life is gone and this signifies that all of our past has been resolved because we accept the plan of salvation.

It is never wise to establish a doctrine on a verse isolated out of its context. In this case, Paul notes that Christ died for everyone; for this reason our relationship with those who have become believers in Jesus should be based on that decision, not on their appearance or on their former reputations. He was emphasizing the importance of breaking down barriers and avoiding prejudice when dealing with new believers; we need to know them from the perspective of the new birth, not according to their flesh.

A better and more contemporary way we can understand this text would be the appearance at our church of a biker-type, skinhead, tattooed fellow, full of piercings who just looks mean and intimidating. He is saved during the church service. How will we relate to this person – with reservations or with open hospitality?

Deliverance is a part of the regenerative process of a soul undergoing sanctification and becoming fruitful. It is not completed in the experience of the new birth. The new birth brings a divine protection and a new perspective of life, but it does not automatically cancel nor totally isolate curses or spiritual attacks, sickness, infirmities, temptations, debts, bad habits, legal proceedings, etc.

The danger is to use this verse as if the new birth were everything. To tell a person who has just accepted Jesus that now everything in their life is resolved would be to deceive them. It treats very serious situations in a superficial manner. This becomes the pretext for irresponsibility on the part of many, encouraging self-indulgence, the lack of spiritual growth and doctrines that make salvation unconditional. Stated differently, even with the compulsive practice of sin, without spiritual coherence and perseverance, even withholding forgiveness, "once saved always saved" is used as a magical band-aid. This is a disaster! This kind of teaching has transformed many churches into prisons.

As much as people try to maintain an air of spirituality, many of them continue to be involved in serious sins, conflicts of conscience, spiritual attacks, emotional disturbances and depression, relationships in crises and many other symptoms that point to major disorders and strong demonic exploitation. Being taught that once they were saved all of this would be resolved, they lose hope and end up spiritually frustrated. Many remain unfruitful and even end up leaving church; not a few end up giving up on their faith entirely.

Everyone born again has, in Christ, the right to a totally free life. However, there is a spiritual distance between "the right to a free life" and "implementing this right in their life." Every benefit of Jesus' sacrifice needs to be personally received and specifically responded to by the application of the appropriate principles.

Suppose that before accepting Jesus you had a debt with a financial institution. Would the fact that you were born again cancel your debt? You would obviously respond "no." Yet, one could argue: "But hasn't the old life died and everything been made new?" Would the manager of the financial institution agree with me if I said that my debt with him was canceled because I accepted Jesus last Sunday? He would probably laugh at me. The new birth deals with the guilt of the past but does not exempt us from unsettled issues or the consequences of that past, regardless of whether they are material or spiritual.

How do you resolve this? Is it possible that God can overcome this mountain of debt of our past? Yes! He became our Father! With this in our account we go the accounts receivables department and pay the debt. We have the resources; go and pay off the debt. Only then can we be free. This is deliverance – you, using the resources guaranteed by the grace of God in Christ, using the principles implicit in the sacrifice of Jesus to settle each debt, silencing the voice of the creditor and accuser.

Nothing is automatic in the spiritual kingdom. Any action by God is always dependent on a human attitude. Jesus died so everyone could be saved, healed, delivered, sanctified, etc. Will all be saved? No! Only those who respond to the Gospel call and repent. Will everyone be healed of their ills because of their salvation? No! Only those who have, or will receive, faith for this. Has everyone been totally delivered because they have accepted Jesus? Also, no! Are all sanctified by the baptism of the Holy Spirit and fire? If only! The world would have already been evangelized if that were true.

Salvation, in fact, is a defined, instantaneous experience. Upon establishing an alliance with God through the sacrifice of Jesus, our spirit is recreated, i.e., we are born again. The soul, however, is a daily conquest that involves humiliation, restitution, brokenness, surrender, discipline, revelation, discernment, intercession, obedience, perseverance, etc. While we may not like it, these words show us God's path that can lead us to the highest spiritual conquests.

The conquest of the soul is nicely allegorized by the conquest of Canaan. Canaan signifies the promise of an abundant life in Christ. To obtain this, many kings and enemy strongholds must be defeated.

The land needs to be delivered. Joshua, a type of the Holy Spirit, needs to plant his feet in every area of our soul. Everything that we submit to the Holy Spirit is under the redemptive power of the Lord Jesus. Everything that we do not submit to the Holy Spirit continues vulnerable to malignant influences and setbacks.

4. THREE ASPECTS OF RESTORATION

1) Regeneration
Regeneration is the process of being created again by a new Spirit and new values. In practice, I understand this covers the process of evangelization, the new birth and discipleship until the person can establish a real commitment to the values of the Kingdom of God and is capable of developing a "personal devotional life."

"...throw off your old sinful nature and your former way of life, which is corrupted by lust and deception. Instead, let

the Spirit renew your thoughts and attitudes. Put on your new nature, created to be like God—truly righteous and holy. So stop telling lies. Let us tell our neighbors the truth, for we are all parts of the same body. And "don't sin by letting anger control you." Don't let the sun go down while you are still angry, for anger gives a foothold to the devil. If you are a thief, quit stealing..." (Ep 4:22-28).

We can establish two important practices of regeneration:

• **Throw off the old man and put on the new.** This is an exchange of values and procedures that does justice to the new birth. The Bible does not say that we can throw off the old demons. This is not the question. Demonic exploitation is always the side effect of human corruption. It is essential to the transformation of values. You cannot transform a person or deal with their spiritual problems without changing their values.

• **Do not give a foothold to the devil.** Simultaneously, after throwing off the old man and putting on the new, the apostle Paul warns that we should not give a foothold to the devil. We cannot separate our values and behavior from the respective spiritual influence. Note that these admonitions were made to *"God's holy people in Ephesus, who are faithful followers of Christ Jesus" (Ep 1:1).*

According to the context of the church in Ephesus, when you allow a situation to exist where anger, lying, stealing, etc., are out of control, it becomes the legal jurisdiction of Satan in the life of the *"faithful"* in Christ (Ep 1:1). These doors of mismanagement need to be closed. The concept of spiritual deliverance and maturity are based on the exercise of self-control as the fruit of our relationship with God.

2) Deliverance

Deliverance can be better stated as the "model of deliverance counseling." It is specific advice, intelligently applying the knowledge and power of the sacrifice of Jesus Christ, dealing with one's personal, generational and territorial "history," and addressing the "lifestyle

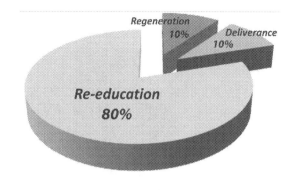

of the person in question. Deliverance accounts for 10% of the sanctification process. Deliverance is fundamental, but it is not everything. It should be emphasized in the right proportions. It is important to keep in mind that the emphasis of this book is on this 10%.

As mentioned earlier, the emphasis of deliverance is not a direct attack on demonic exploitation or the symptoms of latent spiritual attacks; it addresses the root causes: guilt, shame, trauma, resentment, generational iniquities, pacts made through the occult, open doors of carnality involving emotional, sentimental, organic or sexual dependence, etc. This is a fundamental aspect of shepherding.

Deliverance aims to "reset" all the accumulated personal and generational (inherited) injustice. It is the process of nullifying any possibility of satanic accusation or spiritual attack; it cultivates a rich spiritual atmosphere. This is what many naively think happens as a result of the new birth. Deliverance wisely administered, in a genuinely regenerated person, is a turning point in their life.

3) Re-education

The goal of re-education is to dismantle those areas of one's life that have been marked by sin and failure and reconstruct a style of life permeated by obedience. Without a doubt, this is the hardest part. The greatest challenge lies in the re-education of the identity (spiritual, sexual, vocational, etc.), in the reintegration of the personality, in the dismantling of the soul's relationship to the emotional, moral, rational structures and sophistries it has created and in the change of habits and the abandonment of addictions, etc. The deliverance process that ignores the re-education of the soul becomes irresponsible and ineffective. It is at this point that regeneration begins in earnest, where "the rubber meets the road." We can better understand the re-education process through three positions that should be a part of our "following-Jesus" lifestyle:

• *Learn to unlearn*. Eliminate arguments and reasoning that are contrary to the wisdom of God and that imprison our soul. There must be an emotional and moral de-conditioning regarding bad habits, bad attitudes and false ideologies. This is a process of detachment or de-possession. These are internal changes that directly affect the lifestyle:

> *"So get rid of all the filth and evil in your lives, and humbly accept the word God has planted in your hearts, for it has the power to save your souls" (Ja 1:21).*

Wounds in the soul create a terrific opportunity for speculation and reasoning to implement evil. These arguments are interpreted by the apostle Paul as a "fortress of the mind," i.e., "a prison built by thoughts." Soul prisons are evil thoughts that are created through wounds and wrongs. It is not enough to treat the wounds; the thought process itself that is contrary to the mind of Christ must be confronted. Otherwise it has the power to keep the various aspects of life and relationships in captivity. These are thoughts based on intolerance, violence, bitterness, sarcasm, scorn, isolation, inferiority, pride, religiosity, denominationalism, etc.

We need to learn to unlearn these ideologies. To do this, a daily devotional relationship with the Word of God is vital. Such a relationship can produce very surprising results.

• *Learn to relearn*. Be open to new concepts and values that brings us closer to God and reconciles us with others. This is the essence of brokenness. To relearn is to learn again. This requires patience and much humility. In a world where everyone errs, the greatest virtue is the capacity to accept correction. This is a psycho-therapeutic process that enhances the quality of life.

• *Learn to keep learning*. A lifestyle of humility, discipline and wisdom needs to be preserved. Be in a state of constantly learning, from everything and everybody, always demonstrating gratitude. This is a life that grows in the grace and knowledge of the Lord Jesus. The greatest and most valuable lessons come from sources that disparage; it also shows the danger of the maturity syndrome – people learn to

2

COUNSELING AND DELIVERANCE

Everyone has a story and a character, or rather, a past and a present, which needs to be redeemed. Although one's story (familial, generational and territorial) does not necessarily determine the character of an individual, it does exert an influence that should not be underestimated. Our historical background determines our culture, which determines who we are, and sustains spiritual powers that are capable of dictating the direction of a society, whether educating it or imprisoning it in ignorance.

In the Western church we place a high value on behavior while ignoring our spiritual heritage. The result is a barrier that significantly limits our spiritual perception and emasculates our ability to engage in effective spiritual counseling. It is an enormous mistake to discard this spiritual history; it is extremely rich in information. We simply cannot afford to treat the traumas and iniquities we have experienced, and the resulting influence they exert over our choices and decisions, superficially. Successful intercession demands that we target them.

We are charged with the priestly role of diagnosing, confronting and resolving the wounds and iniquities that result from a present lifestyle that is molded by a distorted view of our past history. Applying Gospel values to bring about a proper understanding of the past experiences and the present problems is the ultimate goal of deliverance. Following this model enables us to restore a person to solid spiritual health and encourage an evolving, active faith.

RECONCILING RESPONSIBILITY AND HERITAGE

The first thing that needs to be understood in this model of deliverance is that we cannot separate counseling from deliverance[1]. It is at this point that we break with the popular model of deliverance that emphasizes "power praying" and exorcising or breaking malignant oppression. I am not denigrating the power of a prayer of faith that is inspired by God; however, in practical terms in the majority of cases, this only superficially touches on our true objective. Deliverance requires quality time, i.e., it involves an intelligent spiritual dialogue that is in-depth and unhurried. This is essential if one is to lead a person to an effective application of the biblical principles of deliverance.

Any attempt at spiritual counseling that removes the principles of deliverance is inefficient and any attempt at deliverance without the wisdom of spiritual counseling can become a demonstration of spiritual terrorism and legalism. To deny or neglect the principles of deliverance in discipling will only bring about frustration and, in time, place an inordinate value on these very principles to the detriment of proper choice, an unhealthy spiritual life, mysticism and scandal. The ability to recognize and reconcile the biblical principles of these two issues will create a synergy between them that will result in effective solutions.

Spiritual counseling is fundamental to the process of creating an empathetic interaction with a person who needs help and requires personal confrontation, whether in regards to delicate situations involving trauma or situations involving grotesque sin. It is equally necessary in the post-deliverance process of promoting reeducation in lifestyle choices, especially in those fragile areas of past trauma, and in disciplining the will.

Deliverance focuses on the capacity we have to deal with spiritual attacks that gain strength through the accumulation of generational, territorial and personal injustices by way of the redemptive principles implicit in the sacrifice of Jesus. Human behavior tends to be a reflex of the spiritual influences that accompany us.

---

[1] The word "deliverance" carries much baggage in the American church. It is simultaneously denigrated and embraced by those on opposite sides of the church spectrum. Unfortunately, both extremes generate biases that diminish its biblical perspective. Instead of using a different term that is synonymously interchangeable that might allow us to read the text without superimposing our biases on it, the translation is faithful to the original Portuguese text and uses "deliverance;" the prayer is that it helps to resuscitate an important biblical word and concept that helps the church to become stronger.

I must admit that in the beginning of my ministry I encountered many situations that quite literally drained my repertory of counseling skills without helping the person move one inch out of their conflict. As a result,

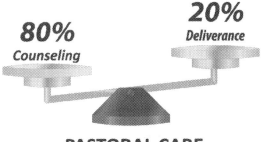

80% *Counseling*

20% *Deliverance*

PASTORAL CARE

I became convinced that any spiritual counseling that ignores the biblical principles of deliverance ends up becoming a victim of a scarcity of results in most situations.

On one occasion, after an extremely long and exhausting counseling session in a critical marital situation, I perceived that things were getting worse instead of improving. Already completely drained, not knowing what else to argue or do, my frustration and sense of failure was so great that I told the couple: "I've never counseled a couple to separate and will never do this, however, if you separate, I will understand." That was my declaration of defeat with which I closed my participation in the case. Today I look at that situation with regret because now I know exactly how to better help them.

Spiritual counseling and deliverance need to walk together so that the ministry of restoration is not positioned in the extremes that unbalance our potential to help. In many complicated cases involving homosexuality, adultery, nervous breakdowns, dysfunctional families, Satanism or serious situations that imply a demonic infestation, if we do not take the path of deliverance, we will end up imploding the whole spiritual counseling process into an empty management of the situation without results.

To improve the effectiveness of the spiritual counseling model in deliverance, it is important to establish that, generally speaking, pastoral care dictates that 80 to 90% of all effort involves counseling and 10 to 20% involves deliverance.

It is fundamental that we proceed simultaneously in both spiritual counseling and deliverance. In practice, you cannot separate the two; however, from a didactic perspective, we will attempt to isolate the two concepts.

SPIRITUAL COUNSELING – emphasizes the law of responsibility

Spiritual counseling is primarily concerned with psychosomatic issues. A psycho-somatic disorder can be defined as a problem of the soul (psycho) that reflects in the body (soma), producing organic dysfunctions and illnesses for which a cure that is merely chemical does not exist.

It is stated scientifically that 80% of illnesses like digestive problems, ulcers, headaches, allergies, etc., are psychosomatic in nature. Behind these illnesses exists chronic emotional behaviors of anxiety, insecurity, fear, guilt, shame, etc., that are basically supported by emotional pain that is related to rejection and emotional wounds. Thus, it is more important that you know "what type of person has an illness" than "what type of illness has a person." It is precisely in these cases that drugs serve merely to treat the collateral organic effects without interacting with the true causes that are primarily of a spiritual nature, secondarily of a psychosomatic nature and finally are actually organic in various pathologies.

Underneath a psychosomatic disorder there is usually a basis of rejection and abuse. However, the more important aspect is not the rejection nor the wrongs suffered, rather, the choices we made because of them. It does not matter what they did to us; more important is what we are doing with what they did to us. Our choices build habits that define our character and determine our destiny. This is the law of responsibility. We cannot justify our moral irresponsibility based on rejections or inherited influences; or stated in a different fashion, we cannot justify temptation as an excuse to sin.

When one attempts to compensate for an emotional deficit with excessive need, the personality is distorted and internal barriers (strongholds) are generated. The lack of affection only increases the appetite for sin and this leaves a trail of destruction in the personality. It is at this point that spiritual counseling (deliverance) enters, helping diagnose the emotional problems and reasoning that opposes the knowledge of God. It challenges the lifestyle choices and guides the person through the application of true principles and this helps them make the choices that are necessary.

Spiritual counseling produces knowledge. Knowledge produces responsibility. Responsibility produces freedom. The more intelligent and prophetic the counseling is, the greater the knowledge and the light the person receives to organize their own life. The greater the light, the greater is his responsibility, and the more responsibility the person embraces, the greater the freedom. There is no freedom without responsibility. This dynamic expresses the power of deliverance.

In some cultures, especially Latin, the concept of freedom is related to comfort and wealth, i.e., a "prosperous tranquility." But in fact, these things do not bring fulfillment nor freedom, but boredom and frustration. True freedom is associated with responsibility.

Spiritual counseling connects the person with the appropriate divine truths. This mechanism enables the renewal of the mind, the undoing of lies, false arguments, cultures and strongholds that enslave and distort their way of thinking and acting. It enables them to responsibly take practical stances that have the power to transform lives and reverse any disastrous situation. The essence of spiritual counseling is to redeem the ability to think and react, through the discernment of truth.

Personal effort and the systemic approach

The diagram below, prepared by Rabbi Edwin H. Friedman[2] and adapted by Steve Reynolds, shows four groups of people along two important axes of life: quality of environment vs. personal response in relationships.

– In the first quadrant: A mature person who is fruitful in a functional environment and has mature emotional responses.

– In the second quadrant: An immature person who, despite being in a functional environment, responds with immaturity in relationships. These are the people who seek counseling and attend therapy rooms.

– In the third quadrant: A mature person who, despite living in a dysfunctional environment, overcomes with resilience and maturity.

– In the fourth quadrant: A very immature person who grew up in a stressful environment and responds immaturely. Many of them become marginalized (homeless, junkies, thieves, etc.).

---

[2]Rabbi Edwin H. Friedman DD - *"The Challenge of Change and the Spirit of Adventure".*

I–VERY MATURE PERSON
--stable
--needs little help
--good family structure
--well-rounded
--responsible
--high functioning

III–MATURE PERSON
--resilient, bounces back quickly
--ability to cooperate
--responds well to challenges
--doesn't let mood get him down, happy
--able to respond with maturity in a toxic environment

The way one reacts is the key to overcome toxic factors

Better   QUALITY OF ENVIRONMENT   Worse

CONDITION

(Low Stress)
Structured environment, healthy, tranquil

(High Stress)
Focus of PATHOGENESIS: origin of disease

II–IMMATURE PERSON
--very passive
--agitated, disturbed
--unstable
--self-condemning
--victim

These are people who seek counseling

IV–VERY IMMATURE PERSON
--homeless
--chronic problems
--abandoned (destitute)
--asylums

Marginalized

100 (Very Mature) Focus of EFFORT

RESPONSE

RESPONSE

(Immature) 0

To address the majority of human problems that we face, we can establish a ratio between the hostility of the environment and personal response (HE / PR), considering factors such as emotional strength, resilience, self-control, hope, etc. Whenever we increase the denominator (personal response), we have a great power to reduce the numerator (hostile environment). When the denominator (personal response) tends to zero, which occurs in passive people, with a position of victim, negative, highly reactive without self-control, so no matter how small the numerator (hostile environment) produces infinite proportions.

In a society oriented toward pathology (science that studies the origin, nature of symptoms and diseases), the tendency is to focus only on the horizontal axis – the condition of the environment. However, human growth, maturity, relationships, social development, and perhaps all long lasting, effectual healing depends on the qualities that are measured by the vertical axis – the response of people in relationships.

Obviously, if your main target is direct social action and transformation of toxic environmental factors, then the horizontal axis is, and should be your priority. But I am talking about a clinical point of view, and in this context, an orientation to the horizontal axis (environmental conditions) greater than the vertical line (personal response) is counter-evolutionary. Otherwise, ignoring the condition of the environment can seriously hamper the expected results in counseling. What is observed in practice is that the person's response depends on the social system where it is assimilated (especially family).

This is the systemic approach to life. For example, an addict after nine months hospitalized in an appropriate environment recovers, but when returned to the old social system (the dysfunctional family), he quickly returns to his addiction. On the other hand, if, besides putting the addict in a recovery program, an effort is also made to work with the family, lowering the environmental stressors and investing in the quality of relationships, when the recovered addict returns home, the chance of failing is much smaller.

In fact, unless the efforts of family members are implemented and promoted, any attempt to improve the environment tends to crumble. In other words, improvements in external family conditions do not last unless there is a corresponding effort on the part of all who are a part of the system. We often see parents who have labeled a rebellious, addicted, etc., child as being the "problem" of the family. However, when you view the issue from a systemic point of view, you realize that he was nothing more than the result of a highly stressful, dysfunctional family system. Relationships are managed in a totally immature, and often abusive, manner. The very fact that parents blame the "problem" child demonstrates the emotional deficiency in the system. The healing process must be focused as much on the person who needs healing (the addicted person) as on the healer (the dysfunctional family). Once the restoration process moves the person along the vertical axis, everyone can grow in maturity. To maximize the potential of spiritual counseling, we should work on both axes, first increasing maturity but also reducing the stress of the environment.

DELIVERANCE – emphasizes the law of inheritance

Psychology, despite crushing the emotional past of people, ignores the spiritual principles of redemption. Similarly, psychiatry, which only combats the biochemical disorders of the body, in most cases, does not interact with the real causes of emotional disturbances. Without criticizing the positive aspects of psychology and psychiatry, any science that sins against the discernment of the spirit world is a double-edged sword. On the one hand it can help, and on the other it is inefficient, and even harmful.

In the area of deliverance we are basically dealing with the evils of "pneumopsychosomatic" (pneuma = spirit, psycho = soul and soma = body). This is a terminology that I created in an attempt to define the spiritual issues that touch the emotional, psychological and physical. This is the missing link of psychology and the blind spot of human science. There are evil spirits who infiltrate specific areas of a person's life, due to wounds or inequities of generational or personal origin.

Ignoring the laws that govern the spiritual world is a catastrophic mistake and ignoring their agents worsens the situation. In no way do I want to construct a doctrine of deliverance that gives prominence to demons. This would be tragically superficial. Our biggest problem in spiritual conflict is not the presence of demons, but the absence of God. The issue is that many of us have demons, a definite "foul" against the Holy Spirit in specific areas of our lives. In fact, the whole issue of demonic infestation is nothing more than the side effect of banning the presence of God from our lives. Just as the Word of God only germinates when sown on fertile land, so demons need a mind susceptible to their designs.

Generational inequities, injustices systematically suffered, wounds caused by authorities, sins tied to the process of family formation can all build attitudes that facilitate a strong demonic infiltration. As a result, these demons perform their assignments according to the nature of the breach that allowed their entry. For every sin there is a corresponding evil spirit with that nature. They set up house and torment people, supporting sinful connections and spiritual prisons in the various areas of human life: emotional, financial, sexual, physical, occupational, mental, marital, family, etc.

The Bible tells of several cases that illustrate this. A good example was when Jesus confronted Peter's limitation to forgive, telling the famous parable of the uncompassionate creditor – a man who was forgiven a gargantuan debt but withheld forgiveness in relation to an insignificant debt. Therefore, the lender gets a merciless verdict by offering a grace far short of what he received: Then the angry king sent the man to prison to be tortured until he had paid his entire debt. *"That's what my heavenly Father will do to you if you refuse to forgive your brothers and sisters from your heart." (Mt 18:34,35).*

Jesus exposes the spiritual character of many problems and diseases. He teaches his disciples how unforgiveness invokes the tormentors or "torturing spirits." Literally, these agents perform the task of executioner. Several types of emotional and physical torments are supported by these spirits of distress coming from the wounds of the soul. We have here a situation purely organic or psychological. Accordingly, without this discernment of the spiritual reality, the manner we attempt to intervene becomes irrelevant.

Analyzing an episode of deliverance

To illustrate the importance of acting simultaneously with the principles of spiritual counseling and deliverance, let's consider a biblical episode narrated in the Gospel of Luke:

> *One Sabbath day as Jesus was teaching in a synagogue, he saw a woman who had been crippled by an evil spirit. She had been bent double for eighteen years and was unable to stand up straight. When Jesus saw her, he called her over and said, "Dear woman, you are healed of your sickness!" Then he touched her, and instantly she could stand straight. How she praised God! But the leader in charge of the synagogue was indignant that Jesus had healed her on the Sabbath day. "There are six days of the week for working," he said to the crowd. "Come on those days to be healed, not on the Sabbath." But the Lord replied, "You hypocrites! Each of you works on the Sabbath day! Don't you untie your ox or your donkey from its stall on the Sabbath and lead it out for water? This dear woman, a daughter of Abraham, has been held in bondage by Satan for eighteen years. Isn't it right that she be released, even on the Sabbath?" This shamed his enemies, but all the people rejoiced at the wonderful things he did. (Lk 13:10-17).*

It was a Saturday, a day when people were at church and Jesus ministered. Suddenly, he addresses a woman who was severely bent over and heals her. In narrating the situation, Luke provides a diagnosis. He claims that this woman had a "spirit of infirmity." Being a doctor, a man of science, he makes it clear that the cause of the problem was not physical, but spiritual

It is important to note the manner Jesus refers to this woman, classifying her as a "daughter of Abraham," i.e., a practitioner of the faith, a believer. The main aspect is the diagnosis established by Jesus himself. He reveals that in spite of her faith, this woman for 18 years had been a prisoner of Satan. I imagine that this would appear strange and even shocking to many. Satan held her through a physical deformity! How can a daughter of Abraham, a person legitimately saved, have a spirit of infirmity and be a prisoner of Satan? I know that this does not mesh with the theology that many of us hold. While Jesus confirmed the salvation of the woman, he also stated that a "spirit of infirmity" physically imprisoned her.

Considering the implications of her deformity—living doubled over, crooked, without the ability to straighten up—she was always looking at the floor of life! Here we have the reflection of a person who suffers inwardly. This woman represents a church within the church that suffers spiritually: people who are deformed, warped, looking down at their feet, without any spiritual perspective, licking their wounds, idolizing their own needs. People steeped in inferiority, rejection and hopelessness. I want to emphasize that I am talking about saved people, believers, who are part of the church.

Cases like this are not merely "emotional problems," which can be solved with a simple counseling session or a psychiatric recipe, but rather are demonic situations, literally satanic, which require genuine liberation. This was the unquestionable diagnosis of Jesus himself: *"This dear woman, a daughter of Abraham, has been held in bondage by Satan for eighteen years. Isn't it right that she be released, even on the Sabbath" (Lk 13:16).*

This daughter of Abraham was imprisoned by a spiritual illness that affected not only her self-esteem, but also her objectivity. She lived disfigured. She needed a spiritual deliverance. All the counseling in the world would not be enough to help her. To naturalize situations like this is a mistake. To do so, to simply apply counseling principles, is no better than merely firing a shot in the dark.

We need to understand that this is not just a simple episode of physical healing. Here we have a practical class in deliverance. Traumas and wounds build strongholds where the enemy attacks us from within, through mental illness and sophistry contrary to divine knowledge, which trap the soul and compromise the ability to develop healthy relationships. This is what Jesus called being in bondage by Satan. It is essential to deal with the residual pain of these wounds, excising the reasoning and habits that have been developed.

Dealing with a wounded memory – inner healing

In truth, that woman's deformity, despite being sustained by the presence of a demonic agent, was caused by a trauma that the text demonstrates existed. The spirit of infirmity was merely a parasite in a situation that was unresolved.

Jesus deepened the process by publicly disclosing the age of the trauma. This was highly strategic. She had been imprisoned by Satan for 18 years. He was not merely acknowledging the murmurings of the religious; rather, he was surgically uncovering the specific act that caused her spiritual imprisonment. Additionally, it was more than a spiritual revelation about the cause of the problem; Jesus was confronting the way the woman had been dealing with this reality.

Jesus was dealing with her wound surgically. At that moment, seeing herself face to face with the situation 18 years prior, her memory burned with pain, fear and other disturbing feelings and constraints. By dating the trauma, Jesus activated her memory, leading her to confront the source of the evil, but with the spiritual resources that He was providing. She was given the vivid opportunity to finally, with the grace offered by God, disconnect her life from that "present past," so she would never have to relive it again.

A major source of feedback is the memory of the soul. As much as the memory can make use of "subconscious" mechanisms, it is basically an element connected to our consciousness, where the records of every event in our history are stored. Personally, I am not fond of the terms "subconscious" or "unconscious" because they can be interpreted in a dangerous manner to the detriment of the principal moral aspect of humans—personal responsibility. The Bible simply states that humans are conscious beings, not subconscious or unconscious. In fact, these terminologies are not found in the Bible.

So when I refer to inner healing, I am emphasizing the redemption of this wounded memory. This is the product of a set of actions performed intentionally, with emotional intelligence, spiritual discernment, and above all, self-control. From this perspective, I want to list the fundamental principles that enable us to intelligently affect the clinical process of healing the soul.

Basic principles in the process of inner healing

• Revelation / confrontation. People with a sick soul need to confront their memory and history. Our experience has shown us that it is God himself who is the great specialist at treating a person's wounds, precisely because Jesus has already dealt with these hurts through his sacrifice. Many have accepted this confrontation and have ended up encountering the supernatural love of the Father. Teaching, prayers and acts of reconciliation of a priestly nature (that are representative in nature) can be highly strategic and therapeutic tools to channel an anointing that confronts the traumas and reveals the unknown.

• Confession of guilt and shame. This is the biblical way to break the power of a trauma. Amazingly, the way to remove the emotional muzzle of trauma is not to protect yourself, rather to expose yourself to it. The barrier to the healing of one's memories is the reputation that those memories carry, i.e., the pain of shame that is attached to them. The primary evidence of a person who has been delivered or healed internally is their ability to talk about their history with good humor.

• Unconditionally forgive the injustices and rejections that were suffered. It is essential to apply forgiveness profoundly and resolutely. The irrevocable decision to forgive, in conjunction with the removal of the right of a demon to be present, is highly restorative.

• Assume responsibility for wrong choices made that were based on the trauma. Determine to no longer react in the old manner. Change the way you think and react to the injustice you experienced. This is where the transforming power of repentance is experienced.

• Unilaterally reconcile with the person(s) who wounded you. Act with compassion and mercy.

- Intercessorially confess the sins and injustices of those who have hurt you. This will extinguish, or at least significantly lessen, demonic exploitation of the situation. In turn, this will enable an intervention of God in their lives that can lead to their salvation. The nature of the battle is not against flesh and blood; it is a fight of faith.

Definition

With all of this being said we can summarize the concept of inner healing. I need to put several brackets in this definition to broaden the understanding of it. *Inner healing is when someone consciously* (the spirit of the prophet is subject to the prophet), *backed by spiritual maturity gained, with a clear awareness of the gracious presence of God, can face his past* (I prefer the term "face the past" over "back in the past" – "face" means to confront, eliminating the possibility of a regression, which is a mechanism of hypnosis), *being brought to interact* (through a personal experience with God or acts of creative and prophetic intercession) *with the wounded memory* (situations remembered with paralyzing shame, guilt, fear and pain), *dealing with these situations with the principles implicit in Jesus' sacrifice* (humiliation, confession, forgiveness, restitution, intercession, etc.).

BIBLICAL PROPORTIONS

Since we work extensively with the concept of spiritual heritage, it is important to establish the proportions found in the Bible about two concepts: Inheritance and Responsibility. Whenever we deal with a subject that gives a disproportionate emphasis to a biblical declaration, we create an unbalanced teaching. Comparatively, we can broadly say that the biblical emphasis on personal responsibility is 70% while on inheritance it is 30%.

In practice, responsibility and inheritance are principles that are implicit in each other. They are inseparable. Every personal choice generates consequences that are of a collective nature.

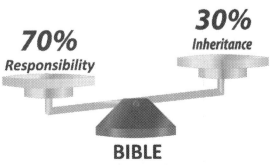

70%
Responsibility

30%
Inheritance

BIBLE

The personal affects the collective and the collective influences the personal. This is the active ingredient to building a culture. It is what science defines as the principle of shared responsibility. The essence of responsibility is choice; the essence of inheritance is influence. An influence is not an obligation. Character, destiny and life are built by choices.

Basically we have two types of choice: "... I have given you the choice between life and death, between blessings and curses. Now I call on heaven and earth to witness the choice you make. Oh, that you would choose life, so that you and your descendants might live!" (Dt 30:19). We either choose obedience, which produces life and prosperity, or we choose sin, which produces death and punishment in the form of various misfortunes and persecutions.

- Obedience makes a claim of justice from a personal perspective (... so that you ...) and an accumulation of promises from a generational perspective (... and your descendants). The Bible mentions that, as Abraham believed God, it was credited to him as righteousness. This credit of justice resulted in a surplus of promises that included himself and all his descendants.

- Sin produces a credit of injustice, i.e., personal guilt, and also spiritual persecution of a collective character, i.e., a generational consequence or an inherited influence. Because of Adam's sin, death was passed on to all men. The whole human race was affected.

Obviously, personal responsibility holds greater importance than our spiritual inheritance. In Hebrew culture the law of inheritance has always been highly regarded, even exaggeratedly so. Yet, we cannot use our generational sin as the excuse for our moral irresponsibility. This type of extreme position is strongly condemned by the prophet Ezekiel (chapter 18). The reality is that in our Western Christian culture, the law of inheritance has lost its meaning and has resulted in a deformed theological and biblical worldview that is limited to redemption and ignores any generational sin connection.

3

SITUATIONS THAT
HINDER DELIVERANCE

Before proceeding to a more effective deliverance it is important to properly assess the regeneration process experienced by the candidate. The symptoms exhibited by a person who has been genuinely born again are very characteristic: sensitivity to sin, spiritual appetite, a desire to witness about his faith, open to communion, etc.

In understanding how the restoration process works, it is fundamentally important that we establish some prerequisites so that the person does not become a victim of a premature deliverance that can be highly irresponsible. When you deal with these prerequisites you are actually beginning the deliverance process.

A premature deliverance can cause more harm than good. When deliverance does not match an attitude of understanding with obedience it can cause the second state of the person to become worse than the first:

> *"If they have escaped the corruption of the world by knowing our Lord and Savior Jesus Christ and are again entangled in it and are overcome, they are worse off at the end than they were at the beginning" (2 Pe 2:20).*

This can be highly destructive and rather than help it can further worsen the person's situation. We need to be aware of some of the situations that common sense can lead us to avoid so we do not hinder a person's deliverance.

It is necessary to build a spiritual foundation in the person's life that will serve as the basis for a successful deliverance. This needs to be done prior to the deliverance, not afterwards. So, I want to list some of the situations that can interfere with our model of spiritual counseling for deliverance.

1. People who are non-believers

The largest cross we have to bear in deliverance ministry is that we often know how to liberate the person but are not able to do so. As long as the person has not taken a clear position in relation to Christ, has not experienced the new birth, is not showing clear evidences of regeneration and commitment to God, we should not be assisting someone with the process of deliverance.

The maximum we can offer is evangelistic counseling. Every deliverance involves a spiritual collision with demonic forces. You do not want to subject the person to such a collision without them first being under the spiritual protection that comes with the certainty of salvation.

We should only expel demons from a non-believer with the proposition of evangelizing them. If they do not want a commitment to Jesus, under no circumstances should we insist, or assist, in the deliverance process. As incredible as it seems, some people do not want to give up the supposed protection they have that comes from demons masquerading as the saints, guides or angels they worship. Without the clear intention of renouncing their lifestyle that serves these entities and committing their life to Jesus, there is nothing we can do other than alerting them to their dangerous spiritual situation.

2. People recently converted to the gospel

What we have often observed in practice is that a premature deliverance ends up causing a loss of faith. Just as important as the freedom that deliverance brings is the ability to maintain it. It is necessary to be consistent and patient in responsibly building a character based on obedience in the very areas where the person had a history of failures and moral wounds. New converts typically do not yet have the understanding and spiritual acumen necessary to support the rigors of an intense deliverance.

Normally, demons that leave will return again with reinforcements (seven worse spirits), to try to reconquer the lost territory. This is where the excitement of the person disappears and they find themselves in a race they cannot win. Many end up lowering their guard and not a few even abandon the faith.

The vast experience of many deliverance counselors teaches us that every neophyte in the faith should undergo discipling for six to twelve months prior to attempting an intense deliverance process. What can be done before this is possible is "first-aid" in areas that are causing disruptions or extreme oppression for the person. Even this process needs to have a foundation laid with much teaching and enlightenment of the direction to be taken in order to create responsibility and sustainability on their part.

3. People not involved with the gospel

In these days when becoming an evangelical has become the fashion, there are many superficial, frivolous people who are only interested in the benefits of the gospel and not a lifestyle of following Jesus. People who do not have a frank willingness to turn from sin are disqualified from going through a process of deliverance. In fact, what these people need is a process of re-evangelization.

We should only allow those committed to the truth and whose life is undergoing a discipling process to undergo an intense action of liberation. Deliverance is only for people who are under the lordship of Jesus and who are genuinely seeking Him. Without this foundation, deliverance can boomerang on them and become a condemnation against them.

4. People who have not been baptized

Baptism not only provides a solid sense of belonging but a sense of having a spiritual paternity. The person is given a benchmark of leadership, church, identity and denominational heritage and a vision of the body. All of this is indispensable for anyone who wants to take seriously the life of a disciple.

To have authority we need to be under authority. Baptism as a public testimony of our faith liberates the boldness of the Holy Spirit to be His witnesses. The most significant characteristic of someone who has experienced the new birth is the freedom to publicly testify of Jesus. Baptism also promotes an understanding of the body and unity in diversity, which in turn provides spiritual protection and authority.

If a person has not been baptized it is important to work on this issue. There may be embarrassment and even personal trauma with respect to having a closer relationship with a community or leadership. It is essential to address these issues, confronting the problem, through specific counseling before proceeding.

5. People who are not congregating

This is an extension of the previous point. These people are without spiritual coverage, mentor or counselor who will accompany them through the deliverance process. In fact, we cannot belong to Jesus and not be a part of the body of Jesus – the church. We all need congregational ties. Isolation ("I only want Jesus, not the church") sins against the wisdom of the Body: "Unfriendly people care only about themselves; they lash out at common sense" (Pr 18:1). You often hear phrases like: "I do not submit to men, only to God," "I do not need a church," "The church is a failed institution," etc. This is the voice of a relationship that has failed.

These cases are normally very serious. People who do not congregate are invariably imprisoned by injuries and strong deceptions that have promoted a strong mentality of independence, rejection, bitterness, rebellion and isolation that can jeopardize the results that would be expected through deliverance. Everyone who defends their position of not "going to church" is isolating themselves from the fellowship of the saints and placing themselves at the mercy of strong demonic influence. The first step to destabilize the activity of these demons is to address the roots of this isolation. In the same manner that we are wounded in relationships so we will be healed in relationships.

No one has ever or will ever be healed by isolating themselves. Isolated people, who resist relating significantly to others, need to overcome this difficulty before moving on to participating in a deliverance process. Consistent counseling in this direction is essential. Unless this situation is satisfactorily resolved, deliverance will either have no effect or will bring more harm than good.

6. People who refuse to genuinely forgive someone

The lack of forgiveness in the context of deliverance is an unforgivable "sin." It blocks the grace of God and strengths both the chains and the sentence imposed by the "tormentors," as Jesus himself taught. Yet, some people persist in living in bitterness and disappointment.

When we find that the person does not intend to forgive anyone, we interrupt the deliverance process and switch to a counseling mode until we are able to dissuade the person from that stance. If the person definitively refuses to forgive, the process ends there. It is a hard thing to do but unfortunately there is no other option.

It is strategic to begin the deliverance process in the areas of trauma, injustices and abuses that the person has suffered. Many of the demonic influences that are sustaining the most terrible panoramas of persecution and affliction are being sheltered and fed by resentment, bitterness, hatred and indifference that the person is nurturing in relation to their abusers. If they refuse to forgive their aggressors, there is nothing more to be done.

7. People who are living together or are dating in an "unequally yoked" situation

Every situation that supports a sin in opposition to the covenant prevents a deliverance from occurring. God has no commitment to the uncompromising and frivolous. He is a God of covenant. The very concept of curse is embedded in the breach of the covenant. There is no way to crucify the curse of a person who remains in a state of that curse.

Unfortunately, churches are infested with people who are living together, including people in positions of leadership. Few people care to broach this subject, but it is a common reality. People living together should be wisely guided to resolve this situation. Basically there are two alternatives: either marry or separate. Some parameters will weigh heavily on this decision: if the other person is a believer or not, the existence of a child, financial dependence, time of living together, etc. This can become a different equation for each type of situation and not a simple one to solve; it will require pastoral visits, prayer, evangelism, counseling, etc.

Unequally yoked dating should be terminated regardless of the circumstances. Either choose the relationship or choose Jesus. There is no way to simultaneously choose both. I always advise the person to let "Lazarus" die. If in the future, that person was to accept Jesus, and God wants to resurrect "Lazarus," then that is a different story.

One danger here is the other person becoming a "convert" because of the person they like, becoming a wolf in sheep's clothing. When this happens—invariably after the wedding—the wolf strips off the sheepskin and it is too late. Soon passion turns to betrayal, disappointment and even disgust. The unequally yoked scenario always brings much spiritual oppression and family suffering.

Part II

Analyzing the Diagram of the Model of Deliverance Counseling

Diagram of the Model of Deliverance Counseling

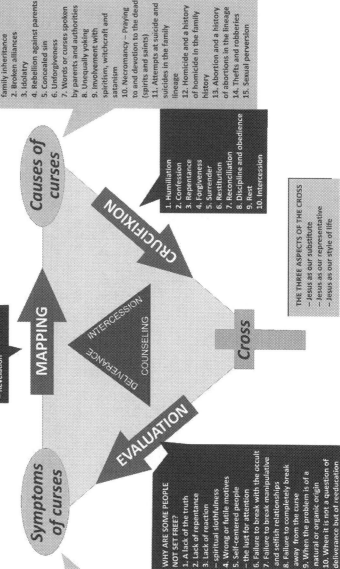

Causes of curses

1. Sins of the parents – family inheritance
2. Broken alliances
3. Idolatry
4. Rebellion against parents
5. Concealed sin
6. Unforgiveness
7. Words or curses spoken by parents and authorities
8. Unequally yoking
9. Involvement with spiritism, witchcraft and satanism
10. Necromancy – Praying to and devotion to the dead (spirits and saints)
11. Attempts at suicide and suicides in the family lineage
12. Homicide and a history of homicide in the family history
13. Abortion and a history of abortions in the lineage
14. Thefts and robberies
15. Sexual perversion

CRUCIFIXION

1. Humiliation
2. Confession
3. Repentance
4. Forgiveness
5. Surrender
6. Restitution
7. Reconciliation
8. Discipline and obedience
9. Rest
10. Intercession

MAPPING

– Research and interview
– Revelation

INTERCESSION
DELIVERANCE
COUNSELING

Cross

THE THREE ASPECTS OF THE CROSS
– Jesus as our substitute
– Jesus as our representative
– Jesus as our style of life

EVALUATION

WHY ARE SOME PEOPLE NOT SET FREE?
1. A lack of the truth
2. Lack of repentance
3. Lack of reaction – spiritual slothfulness
4. Wrong or futile motives – the lust for attention
5. Self-centered people
6. Failure to break with the occult
7. Failure to break manipulative and selfish relationships
8. Failure to completely break away from the curse
9. When the problem is of a natural or organic origin
10. When it is not a question of deliverance but of reeducation

Symptoms of curses

1. When the person is "serving God" with spiritualist gifts
2. Chronic or repeated diseases without clear medical diagnosis, especially if they are of a hereditary character
3. Chronic sterility
4. Family disintegration
5. Chronic economic failure, especially when income seems to be sufficient
6. Chronic situations of sudden losses, accidents and frequent surgeries
7. Chronic failure associated with a family history of suicide
8. Unrestrained anger associated with a family history of homicides and crime
9. Chronic or cyclical insanity and mental breakdowns
10. Periods of childhood memory that have been erased and impulsive tendencies
11. Transference of family behaviors and addictions
12. Familial history of chronic premature deaths, widowhood and loss of children
13. Sinful connections of a hereditary character
14. Abnormal sexual problems and deviations

Analyzing the diagram

The diagram on deliverance is simply a map by which we logically and sequentially build the process of deliverance by bringing together the relevant principles. Each part of this diagram is essential. Each point and each distance travelled are essential for the final result. As we look at this diagram, we will discover that minor flaws or major negligence can seriously compromise the entire process.

All disease implies three basic situations: the symptoms, the causes and the treatment:

• The *symptom* is the alert mechanism. It indicates the existence of any disorder in that organism. Whether it is a physical pain, an emotional depression, a spiritual attack, etc., these things themselves are not the problem; they are only alerting us of the problem.

• The *cause* is the dysfunction itself, the true source of the problem. It is what needs to be discovered and attacked. It is typically multi-factorial.

• The *treatment* is the path to resolving the problem. It is the cure and the therapy that is associated with a specific solution that needs to be provided by way of a correct diagnosis.

There is an intelligent relationship between the symptom, the cause and the cure of pneumo-psycho-somatic ills that needs to be understood. Connecting these three elements in the proper manner is vital to the restoration process. This is the reason I developed the "Deliverance Diagram." There is a need for a model of spiritual counseling that is both easy to follow and functional. It can be used to examine and solve the most diverse situations that any therapist of the soul might face.

This diagram lays out three points that need to be well defined and elaborated in each person's specific situation:

1. Latent symptoms of curses
2. Respective causes
3. The cross of Christ

It also establishes three distances that need to be fully covered:

1. The process of mapping
2. The process of crucifixion
3. The process of evaluation

Briefly describing the diagram, it is first essential to pay attention to the symptoms of curses by listening to the person. Their existence point to the primary causes from which a person needs deliverance. The manner these complaints are verbalized usually represent the very symptoms of a curse or spiritual attack.

Noting the relevance of the symptoms of any curse that is present, the next step is to find the causes. The same is true if symptoms of a spiritual attack are present. However, as the diagram shows, there is a spiritual distance between symptoms and causes. This distance can signify, depending on the situation, that an easy path can be

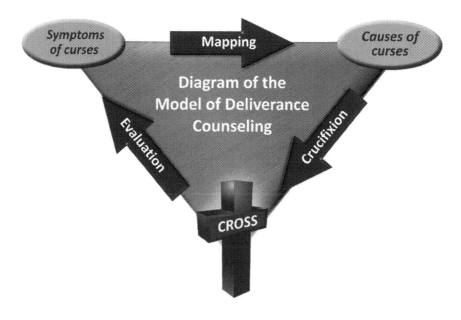

taken or that a darker, more difficult one must be traveled. Spiritual mapping is the tool that determines the path to be taken. The causes of spiritual disorders are usually related to hidden sins, carnal and passive lifestyles, generational and/or territorial inequalities, wounds, abuse, blame, shame, enmities, barriers, etc.

Similarly, just as there is a spiritual distance between the symptoms and causes, there is also a distance between the causes and cure. All diagnosis requires a proper medication. Spiritually speaking, healing is based on the cross of Christ. The sacrifice of Jesus means forgiveness for sins, healing for wounds, deliverance from curses, etc. It is essential in counseling to cover this distance between the causes of a curse and the cross of Christ. Once the causes are established, then comes the painful process of crucifying them without avoiding any of the genuinely viable and necessary alternatives. The process of crucifixion is based on the principles of transparency and reconciliation:

> "But if we are living in the light, as God is in the light, then we have fellowship with each other, and the blood of Jesus, his Son, cleanses us from all sin." (1 Jo 1:7).

The basic context here is not forgiveness; it is purification. Purification goes well beyond being forgiven – it means that you have exhausted every resource to expose, resolve, treat and fix the situation. Only in this way is the blood of Jesus glorified in our lives, eliminating all spiritual contamination.

Transparency and reconciliation unfold in the fundamental principles of the Kingdom of God for human redemption, such as: humiliation, brokenness, confession, resignation, repentance, restitution, forgiveness, reconciliation, obedience, etc. The exercise of these principles is, in fact, what causes a genuine identification with the sacrifice of Jesus, invoking their benefits. This is the correct way to apply the blood of Jesus. Without the exercise of these principles, it does not work. There is no benefit in verbally affirming the power of the blood of Jesus if you are not exercising transparency and reconciliation while facing their spiritual maladies. The process of healing and purification is conditioned by the exercise of these principles.

This distance between the cause of a curse and the cross of Christ must be covered. There is no other option. It is here that the sacrifice of Jesus prevails, supernaturally restoring the spiritual life of the person and establishing a new heaven over him.

Finally, there is the evaluation process where we compare the initial symptoms with the symptoms that are still present after the attempted deliverance. There is always a return to the mapping process and crucifixion to resolve any residual symptom.

It is important to mention that in the deliverance process we are not looking for efficiency, but effectiveness. We cannot be prisoners to time. The model of deliverance counseling requires quality care that can last for several hours. There is no way that a deliverance can take place in 15 minutes or with just one prayer, whether it is powerful or not. It is not that we should not pray for people, but we should not call this deliverance. This will only produce frustration. It is like going to the doctor and getting a prescription without him even looking at you. If we do not have the time needed, it is best to leave it for another time.

Following the diagram, we will consider each point and distance, looking at the most relevant aspects that will help us to build a complete understanding of how to achieve an effective deliverance.

1

SYMPTOMS OF CURSES

If a curse is present, there will be symptoms; the symptoms provide the primary premise for deliverance. We can define symptom as a side effect of the problem. It is not the problem and it is a mistake to interpret it as the problem. Such mistakes frustrate the efforts employed in spiritual counseling.

A correct reading of symptoms is the starting point for an efficient deliverance. The scandalous misfortunes, strange illnesses, uncommon temptations, disturbances and varied attacks of a spiritual or hereditary nature can all characterize what we would define as symptoms of a curse. We need to recognize them to be able to evaluate their real significance. Every symptom carries a message that must be correctly understood. Often this is easily recognizable, on occasions though, we have no clue.

In spiritual counseling we cannot ignore relevant symptoms, but neither should we be looking for unicorns. If there is no clear symptom to investigate, there is no reason to insist on expelling what is not present. On the other hand, if the person has already gone through various deliverance sessions and the symptom of a curse still persists, that is a signal that they still have not dealt with the issues that need to be addressed in spiritual counseling.

The infiltration of curses and demonic exploitation are symptomatic. Each symptom offers a message that should be discerned spiritually and naturally. The key is to not spiritualize the natural and, obviously, to not naturalize the spiritual. This seems simple enough, but, often, it is not. It is in this point that many fall short.

Deliverance is not illiterate; it is necessary to have an intelligent reading of the situation that will enable us to distinguish the real symptoms from the fanciful and unreal. This recognition of the symptoms is the starting point to arrive at the true roots of the problem and develop an efficient process for freedom. Without a good understanding of the symptoms, there is no process/method that will succeed.

Deliverance is also not deaf. It is necessary to sufficiently hear the person and, more importantly, the Holy Spirit. We often attempt to economize time in this area but that is a serious mistake. One unequivocal impression about what is really happening with the person can take us down a totally different path. Normally, when we are not hearing the person, we are also not hearing the Holy Spirit. We have one mouth and two ears – our own anatomy teaches us that we need to hear more and speak less.

To hear something it is necessary to ask something. We need the wisdom of God to intelligently ask questions related to the presented symptoms that will uncover the roots and give clear direction. This is the basis of clinical work.

Here it is important to note that we need to be careful about mysticism. Mysticism's base is speculation and pride. The mystic always offers a corrupted vision and an exaggerated analysis of symptoms, both of which compromise the diagnosis. Without a correct diagnosis, the true causes that sustain the problem will remain untouchable.

EXTREME DANGERS AND DANGEROUS EXTREMES

The greatest enemies on the spiritual battlefield are the extremes that come from an immature understanding. Many neophyte disciples involved in deliverance can subtly or wantonly allow spiritual pride and unbearable legalism to take control. This is how so many have been scandalized in the deliverance process. Becoming the victim, again, the person in need of deliverance becomes antagonistic to the spiritual counseling model, denying that spiritual warfare exists, creating confusion, giving misleading information, becoming critical and divisive and even embracing theological heresies based on differences and frustration. It is important to address the two basic extremes.

1. Spiritualizing the natural
People who are still new in their faith or are emotionally immature tend to overvalue demonic manifestations. They have a

tremendous need to be recognized spiritually and this leads to the danger of becoming victims of false discernment. The supernatural has a way of polarizing people's attention and this can easily lead to the extreme of spiritualizing that which is merely natural.

This can generate spiritual terrorism, encouraged by exaggeration in mystifying everything, and an unfortunate insistence to look for problems where there are none. One's spiritual life becomes a ghost train with demons in every car. This is the type of faith in the enemy that removes God from the picture and ends up giving the devil a dangerous place of authority.

We know that the greatest terrorist in the world is the devil himself. He spreads fear, anxiety and insecurity through his favorite weapon: intimidation. His goal is to undermine faith and spiritual growth. Every Christian practice that puts demonic activities above the greatness of God is potentially unbalanced.

Extremes in relation to "contaminated objects" can also divert our attention from the issues that are really important and create an unbalanced approach that gives poor results. We know about the power of fetishes and magical objects, but to construct a doctrine based on them can produce a legalistic gospel that is based more on fear of the devil than on the freedom to serve God.

God can simply lead us to sanctify the "suspect" objects with prayer: *"Since everything God created is good, we should not reject any of it but receive it with thanks. For we know it is made acceptable by the word of God and prayer" (1 Tm 4:4-5)*. God may lead us to destroy them: *"A number of them who had been practicing sorcery brought their incantation books and burned them at a public bonfire. The value of the books was several million dollars" (At 19:19)*.

There are objects and influences that God can certainly orient us to refute, however, this should happen in a personal manner and under a specific conviction of the Holy Spirit. It is important to not be creating rules and regulations in this sense. It is quite possible that we will end up oppressed, and oppressing, many.

> *"Don't let anyone condemn you by insisting on pious self-denial or the worship of angels, saying they have had visions about these things. Their sinful minds have made them proud, and they are not connected to Christ, the head*

of the body. For he holds the whole body together with its joints and ligaments, and it grows as God nourishes it. You have died with Christ, and he has set you free from the spiritual powers of this world. So why do you keep on following the rules of the world, such as, 'Don't handle! Don't taste! Don't touch!'? Such rules are mere human teachings about things that deteriorate as we use them. These rules may seem wise because they require strong devotion, pious self-denial, and severe bodily discipline. But they provide no help in conquering a person's evil desires" (Co 2:18-23).

God has His hands full when transforming a "natural" man who is completely skeptical into a spiritual person who understands the strong reality of the invisible world. Yet, the task of taking one who is exaggeratedly "spiritual" and transforming them into a "normal" person is even greater. Exaggeration always sins against discernment.

In the text above, Paul labels the motivation of these people who become mystics as carnal, deficient and emotionally unbalanced. This excessive spirituality is fleshly[1] and there is no shortage of spirits of deceit who take advantage of this in order to generate religiosity, confusion and destruction in the church.

2. Naturalizing the spiritual

This position typically develops in reaction to mysticism. Deceptions with mysticism, and the spiritual manipulation of others that accompanies it, can produce chronic skepticism. The principle of unbelief is based in deception. The heart closes. The more some become mystics, the more others become skeptics. Everything begins to be simply analyzed from a natural and psychological perspective. It confines itself to human and theological culture; it is deadly. This is the subtle balance between the letter of the law and the Spirit. Instead of living out the gospel that transforms, we become victims of a rigid theology that deforms.

---

[1] In Colossian 2:18, the Greek is sarkos – "by the mind of his flesh." It could also be translated "by his sinful thoughts," since it appears that Paul is using sarx ("flesh") here in a morally negative way.

Paul warned that the law without the Spirit kills, and that knowledge without love only puffs one up. Jesus also warned that human traditions nullify the commandments of God. We begin to stifle our spiritual life and block our discernment. Pastoral effectiveness is substantially affected.

The result is that in many cases we merely waste our time in exhausting and ineffective counseling sessions.

COMMON SYMPTOMS OF THE EXISTENCE OF CURSES

We should not underestimate the destructive power of sin. Sins and iniquities not redeemed by the sacrifice of Jesus, whether directly related to our ancestry, or us impose a yoke of curses that can easily be identified. In order to better clarify this point on our diagram, I want to present a comprehensive framework of the more common symptoms that indicate the presence of open doors in a person's life that invites attacks.

SYMPTOM 1. Contaminated ministerial gifts – when a person is "serving God" with occultic gifts

I want to give a greater emphasis to this symptom because of the subtleties that are involved. For some this may seem strange or even unacceptable; but, if you study the letters of Jesus to the churches of Asia you will encounter these same situations. He mentions that within the churches were those who were part of the synagogue of Satan (Smyrna), who were participants in the doctrine of Balaam, who followed the doctrine of the Nicolaitans (Pergamum), who were followers of Jezebel (Thyatira), etc.

This infiltration of occultist gifts into the ministry of a church usually comes from a person with a past history of actively practicing, or dabbling in, the occult. It can also be associated with a generational practice of witchcraft.

When we analyze our origins as a nation[2], and how our history unfolded, we notice a heavy load of occultism in our cultural baggage. Our cultural and religious worldview was formed by a syncretism

---

[2] The author is Brazilian.

involving native shamanism, an Islamic-Catholicism from Portugal (syncretized with necromancy and other forms of spiritism), the black magic (quimbanda) of African slaves, French kardecism, etc. All of that has mingled together giving rise to various other religions.

There are three options we can employ to deal with our generational past: the first is to continue to lament our terrible spiritual heritages that were based on immorality, practice of the occult, violence and slavery, and how we were robbed and abused by the settlers of our country. The second is to simply ignore our history and try to row the boat pulling an anchor. Dragging this type of an anchor will dramatically slow us down in the attempt to arrive where we are suppose to be concerning God's purpose for us and it could even cause our efforts to fail. The third option, the only viable one, is to redeem our history, assuming as the church our priestly role: *"They will rebuild the ancient ruins, repairing cities destroyed long ago. They will revive them, though they have been deserted for many generations" (Is 61:4).*

Most of our relatives and ancestors were involved directly or indirectly with the occult. In many families it is possible to perceive a "staff of witchcraft" being passed down from one generation to the next. Despite the label "Catholic, Apostolic, Roman," or "Evangelical," it is easy to find one or more people directly involved with the occult, magic, witchcraft, Satanism, spiritism, secret societies, shamanism, etc.

This has resulted in a latent symptom demonstrated in people who, since infancy, have supernatural gifts like premonition, visions of spirits, hearing voices, out of body experiences (astral projection), divination, incorporation of spirit guides and other forms of mediums. Medium, from Latin meaning "one who is in the middle," is a word used by spiritists to designate people who would be a link between the world of the living and the world of the dead. Strong attractions and strange desires connected to the occult, horror films, witchcraft, contact with the dead and sexual perversion repeatedly affects the person from childhood onward.

Many of these people, in order to "develop," follow the path of occultism in its endless variety of branches, becoming directly involved with demonic entities. The essence of the occult is to receive and handle knowledge, power, pleasure and favor of all species originating from a spiritual source that is demonic, not divine. (For more information I suggest that you read Chapter 6, "Links With the Occult" of my book Roots of Depression).

When these people experience salvation in the person of Jesus Christ, a confrontation starts with all these habits, patterns, gifts, etc., which were received from the occult by either practice or inheritance.

However, the basic question to be addressed with every person who comes from the occult is idolatry of power. In virtually all branches of the occult there is a culture of idolatry of the supernatural that develops, an arrogant feeling of being more "special." This needs to be rigidly repented of and renounced by the person.

It is common to see new converts who came from the occult, even some who occupied priestly positions, quickly establishing themselves as leaders and pastors in a church. They continue to be inspired by the same lust for power that they learned in the occult. If this is not treated, even though their ministry has evangelical trappings, the essence will be occultist.

Therefore, the most important point that needs to be addressed in a person who came from occult practices is idolatry of the lust of power, position and title. This is a subtle way of the enemy to infiltrate the church and usurp and bully divine authority, causing major damage.

Simon Peter vs. Simon the magician

A good biblical example is that of Simon the magician, *"Then Simon himself believed and was baptized. He began following Philip wherever he went, and he was amazed by the signs and great miracles Philip performed" (At 8:13)*. We can see that Simon had a much greater admiration of the "power of God" than for the "person of God." To a certain extent this is natural with new converts, however, later, Simon does not contain himself and attempts, literally, to manipulate and buy this power that he so coveted: *"When Simon saw that the Spirit was given when the apostles laid their hands on people, he offered them money to buy this power" (At 8:18)*. Through this, Peter immediately discerns the malignant infiltration and confronts Simon, going to the true root of his problem – idolatry of power:

"But Peter replied, 'May your money be destroyed with you for thinking God's gift can be bought! You can

have no part in this, for your heart is not right with God. Repent of your wickedness and pray to the Lord. Perhaps he will forgive your evil thoughts, for I can see that you are full of bitter jealousy and are held captive by sin'" (At 8:20-23).

The Bible gives us here a real lesson on deliverance via Peter. Note that Simon had been converted publicly in a major evangelistic crusade of Philip. He had also already been baptized, becoming a part of the church. He became a disciple and supporter of Philip's ministry. He had a great testimony, so much so that his conversion is mentioned in the Bible. He was participating in the ministry of the apostles. However, despite being regarded as a Christian, he continued acting like a sorcerer. Just as he promoted himself by manipulating the power of Satan, he wanted to do the same with the power of God.

I wonder how many "Simons the magician" are inside our churches. We can identify this type of person as one who may be sincere, who is trying to serve God with his ministry, but acting under the inspiration, gifts and mechanisms of witchcraft. As odd as it seems, these people are actually serving God with gifts whose origin is Satan. They are in need of deliverance.

This is very subtle. A person like Simon was so conditioned by the occult that he did not realize that he was subjugated to a malignant motivation (which Peter so adroitly exposes): "full of bitter jealousy" and "held captive by sin." He still needed to remove the bonds of his family inheritances and iniquities that were full of the occult, repenting of his worship of power. This is what definitively accomplishes the deliverance of a person who has roots in the occult. I believe that this intervention of Peter changed the direction of Simon's life and ministry.

Staff or snake?
We see this same type of confrontation with Moses. He was educated in Egypt, a nation steeped in the occult, which idolized death by constructing massive pyramids – tombs or shrines to the spirits of witchcraft and death. This so infected his motivation to help his people that he committed a murder and forced him to flee into a long exile.

After 40 years in the desert under the care of Jethro, working as a shepherd, he receives his calling that comes through a powerful deliverance. It was not easy for God to remove all of Moses' baggage. God not only heals your heart, He purifies your ministry. Without drawing the story out, I want to emphasize the manner in which God reveals to Moses that there was a serious spiritual contamination in the exercise of his ministry.

God orders Moses to throw his staff on the ground and when he does, it becomes a serpent. There was a snake in Moses' staff. It was as if God was saying to him: you are trying to serve me but your ministry is contaminated. There was a demonic infiltration in your pastoral staff. That had to be confronted and defeated. It was necessary for Moses to confront his past of witchcraft, bitterness, and deception that culminated in the murder in Egypt.

The secret of a deliverance ministry is to open the hand that holds the staff, addressing the fascination of power as we saw in Simon's case. Moses had the determination to be the deliverer of the nation. He went so far as to kill for it. His mentality was built by a megalomaniacal culture of occultism. We cannot serve God while building pyramids in our honor. Ministry is service; it is different. Moses wanted the pharaonic power of position. God ordered him: throw down your rod, resign your ministry to Me, give it up, throw out this way of thinking, shake off this yoke. At that moment, when he obeys God's direction to let go of every-thing, the enemy that was in his ministry shows himself. The rod turned into a snake!

Together with God, Moses faces not only his contaminated past and its frustrations but the theophanized demonic principality of Egypt. This demon was now exposed as that serpent through Moses' obedience to God and Moses literally catches him by the tail. His deliverance, and that of all of Israel, began there. Now the serpent became a rod. Moses' ministry, his gift, his calling were all purified, becoming legitimate, devoted only to the living God. With this new staff he became the great deliverer of his nation, performing the wonders of God.

The truth is that many people like Moses are ministering in the church of pastor Jethro, people with a contaminated ministerial gift who need to be delivered. Let's explore this more.

The profane disguised as holy

It is important to distinguish between the holy and the profane. There is a fine line that separates these concepts; they are very similar in appearance but are spiritually conflicting and antagonistic. The issue is that much of Satan's effort focuses on counterfeiting, on camouflage and trying to confuse his ways with the divine.

- *Prophecy vs. divination*

"Then the Lord said, "These prophets are telling lies in my name. I did not send them or tell them to speak. I did not give them any messages. They prophesy of visions and revelations they have never seen or heard. They speak foolishness made up in their own lying hearts" (Je 14:14).

Divinely inspired prophecy always occurs with the motivation and purpose to comfort, edify and encourage. When the essence of a prophet or a prophecy differs from this, the situation has crossed a dangerous line. For this reason every prophecy has to be judged through these five filters: the character of God, God's Word, God's principles, the counsel of God, and, principally, the peace of God.

Amazingly, there is a subtle difference between prophecy and divination, though the prophecy is divine and the divination is demonic. It is common to observe much confusion in churches surrounding the prophetic ministry. Divination is the satanic counterfeit of prophecy, often conveyed by people who have already made a decision for Jesus, are in the church, but who had a history in the occult.

It is interesting to note that in the Afro-Brazilian religious culture, just as there is a false Jesus, Oxalá, a false Mary, Iemanjá, there is also a false Holy Spirit, the Ifã (Python), which is literally the spirit of divination, channeled and consulted by many through the casting of shells, Tarot readings, spirit guide consults, etc.

We can see this discernment between divination and prophecy in this biblical episode:

"Once when we were going to the place of prayer, we were met by a female slave who had a spirit by which she

predicted the future. She earned a great deal of money for her owners by fortune-telling. She followed Paul and the rest of us, shouting, 'These men are servants of the Most High God, who are telling you the way to be saved.' She kept this up for many days. Finally Paul became so annoyed that he turned around and said to the spirit, 'In the name of Jesus Christ I command you to come out of her!' At that moment the spirit left her" (NIV: At 16:16-18).

Despite the fact that the text quickly denounces this young woman as a demon-inhabited medium, Paul only realized it many days later. It is interesting to note how she attended prayer meetings as a believer, even having opportunity to prophesy about the life of Paul and Silas. The contents of her prophecies confirmed actual facts that were encouraging. Though she did not know them, she spoke the truth about who they were. I imagine that in the beginning Paul and Silas might have even felt encouraged by her prophecies and with her ministry.

However, the text says that after a while Paul's spirit was perturbed with the situation. He finally had clear insight about that sister's prophetic ministry. Paul understood in his spirit that the true nature of her prophecies was divination. She was a "Python" believer.[3]

One of the lessons we learn from Paul in this episode is that the motivation of divination is the love of financial gain. The gift is not based on divine inspiration but on the presence of a misleading spirit. This spirit of divination seduces people, causing them to sell their "prophecies" for money. As the text says: *"...earned a great deal of money for her owners by fortune-telling."*

A distinctive feature of a false prophet is a motivation centered on the love of money. His commitment to "money" is greater than his commitment to the "voice of God." Ministerial opportunities are dictated by payment and not by God's direction. This is well illustrated in the story of Balaam, who loved the wages of unrighteousness. A strong indication that a person is a soothsayer and not a prophet is when he focuses his ministry on the rich and important. Other people or churches are treated with total disregard.

---

[3] In the Acts 16:16-18 passage "the spirit by which she predicted the future" is literally translated "spirit of python" in the Greek.

Some Bible translations render the verse: *"a woman who had the spirit of Python,"* to better describe her as a pythoness, a woman possessed of the spirit of divination. Divination flatters and does not encourage or confront; it supernaturally reveals people's past, but the motivation is to lie and manipulate; it is fascinatingly mystical, but empty of genuine spirituality; it does not produce peace before it generates conflict, disruption and deception. These things never end well. This discernment between prophecy and divination can also be expanded conceptually in other ways.

- ### *Hearing the voice of God vs. clairaudience (schizophrenia)*

The Bible speaks of men who heard the voice of God directly from His mouth. Samuel audibly heard God's voice. Similarly, God spoke face to face with Moses. The satanic counterfeiting is known as clairaudience[4] or "clear hearing," when someone starts strangely hearing otherworldly voices. When a person begins to experience this phenomena, they may feel "special, chosen" and it confuses a lot of people who are well intentioned but poorly informed. It invariably becomes a serious disturbance (it is common for people in their occultist involvement to be indoctrinated by their "guides" through auditory and visual contact).

These situations may evolve into a persecution mania, schizophrenia, state of confusion, madness and even suicide and homicide. Recently I visited a young man who was serving a sentence in a sanatorium. I was with the pastor of the church where his mother attended and that he himself had attended. His mother had served demons for many years and after his conversion the son started hearing voices. He told us that the voices told him that he had to kill his mother. Then he told his mother that he loved her but had to kill her and after several attempts to murder her, he ended up being arrested.

This type of symptom has become increasingly common with people who are believers, church people. It is usually associated with a personal and generational past of involvement in the occult. It can also be generated through chronic situations of verbal, physical and sexual abuse. In these cases, a psychiatric approach will merely be

---

[4]The more familiar term clairvoyance, "clear seeing," is used to describe seeing spirits and visions instilled by spirits.

frustrating. In addition to not addressing the real root of the problem, it simply puts the person into a chemical straitjacket through the use of pharmaceuticals in an attempt to control the situation.

• *Prophetic vision vs. the third eye (clairvoyance)*

As the Bible says: *"In those days if people wanted a message from God, they would say, "Let's go and ask the seer," for prophets used to be called seers" (1 Sm 9:9)*. Prophets like Samuel, Elijah and many others had received a legitimate prophetic clairvoyance from God.

The counterfeit of this is known as the opening of the "third eye," "frontal chakra," "mind's eye" or clairvoyance. It is a very common practice within oriental spiritism (China, India, Tibet, etc.), and in new age religions or secret societies like Rosicrucian. This is the ability to see the spiritual world (invisible) through the intervention of a demonic entity. It is the gift of malignantly activated clairvoyance. A person passes through many rituals to reach this level of "illumination." These rituals require the sealing of extremely serious pacts with dark forces of which the participant is typically unaware.

I once was teaching at one of our Youth With a Mission bases. Finishing the first lesson, one of the students approached me, presenting himself as the prophet of his city. He was quite taken with himself, talking continuously about his importance and how he was sought out by pastors in his city and people from his church to receive guidance through his prophecies. It stuck me as sounding very strange. He was quite arrogant and I simply did not pay him much attention.

During the week, the leadership of the course asked me if I would have a counseling session with him. When we sat down, he looked at me and started to fancifully narrate his visions. Honestly, it made my spirit very restless. I am not against prophecies, but I was certain that there was really something wrong with him. Carefully, I changed the course of the conversation and I began to interview him about his life before he knew the gospel. After a few questions, he started to describe, with pride, how he had been involved with the darkness. For many years, he had been a follower of famous witches and had an extensive resume in esotericism and satanism, even outside the country.

I tried to explain that his ministry, despite being something really impressive to many, was contaminated and he had to renounce this open vision that he had of the spiritual world. Immediately he challenged me bluntly, saying: "No! If I do that my ministry will be destroyed!" I explained, in detail, that he was ministering to people not by the Spirit of God, but through occultic gifts. Further, his resistance to renouncing it was justifying his dangerous motivation of idolizing power, the characteristic of a witch and not a prophet. He was reluctant to answer when asked if he had received these gifts before or after his decision to follow Christ. He finally broke and admitted he had received his powers in satanism, well before knowing Jesus.

When we started to pray, he began to renounce the paranormal gifts, the covering of witchcraft and all the rituals that he had participated in to attain those powers. The manifestations accompanying their release were so extremely powerful that it left some of those in attendance terrorized. It was an incredible collision of powers where, once again, the cross of Christ triumphed.

Afterwards, I was thinking about the numerous pastors and people he had taught, prophesied over and laid hands on. What would have been their reaction in light of such a shocking deliverance that he experienced? Unfortunately, he was a warlock with the mantle of a prophet, an open channel for the spirit of divination and control. Despite his sincerity, he was serving God with spiritist gifts.

• Transporting in the spirit vs. astral projection

Transporting in the spirit is a biblical experience experienced by several prophets and apostles.

> "But Elisha asked him, "Don't you realize that I was there in spirit when Naaman stepped down from his chariot to meet you? Is this the time to receive money and clothing, olive groves and vineyards, sheep and cattle, and male and female servants?" (2 Kg 5:26).
>
> "And instantly I was in the Spirit, and I saw a throne in heaven and someone sitting on it" (Re 4:2).
>
> "I was caught up to the third heaven fourteen years ago. Whether I was in my body or out of my body, I don't know—only God knows" (2 Co 12:2).

Astral projection is a satanic way that a person leaves their body, traveling through the spiritual world governed by demons, making pacts, monitoring the lives of people, etc. Some people literally become addicted to it. It is common to attend people who, in certain periods of their lives, have spent more time in the "parallel world" than in the visible world. Astral travel is one of the main elements of witchcraft: "the witch's broom." This is in great fashion at the moment due to its popularity in the Harry Potter movies.

Chatting with a pastor, she began to report something that was happening in her church. Some people at her church were frequently getting together for a "vigil." The issue was that the sole focus of these gatherings was to encourage people to experience an out of body experience or "rapture" as they called it. The truth was that she was frustrated; every time she had participated in these vigils she failed to have any kind of supernatural experience.

I asked her how it took place and she said it happened more or less like this: the leader would tell everyone to lie down and would begin to lead the group in a relaxation exercise, talking to allow the imagination to flow. After this, he would induce a spiritual visualization, telling the participants to "Visualize this … visualize that you are in a particular place," and so on. Many of them would be wrapped up in different experiences of astral projection. Typically, many of the participants had come from the occult, including her own pastor, who led the vigil.

After hearing her experience I told her: "Thank God that you did not have any of those experiences during the vigils!" This was more of a "rupture" experience than a "rapture" experience! In fact, the senior pastor of this church had been living in an adulterous situation for several years and the church was languishing in a series of chronic problems. This is what sets up a church and its leadership for serious symptoms of satanic infiltration through people serving God with gifts that are spiritist or occultic.

One of the strongest cases that I ever attended was of a "leader of intercession and deliverance." Despite the position and ministry that he occupied in his church, his life, marriage and family were on the verge of destruction. I am continuously shocked at how people who do not govern well their own home are irresponsibly placed in leadership positions in the church.

He had many problems; when I looked at the questionnaire he had filled out, I realized that he had been involved with everything you could imagine in the occult. His primary involvement had been in the spiritist religion called *umbanda*[5] where he had competed with other "colleagues" to see who possessed greater power. Very quickly he had received clairvoyance through the indoctrination of his "guide," a spirit who was very accomplished at visualization.

He became very adept at astral projection.

He told me how this "guide" had given him a recipe for a ritual involving candles, aromas and music to facilitate astral projection, making it very easy to come out of his body and visit really strange "planets and places." Forgive me if this sounds like an exaggerated mystic, but I am recounting exactly what he reported.

One day he had an experience that was quite different from his "normal" witchcraft experiences. He challenged his spirit guide to show him how strong he really was. The guide grabbed him by the arm, instantly pulling him into astral projection. Together, traveling at a speed that he had never before experienced on these projections, he found himself going in the direction of a cemetery. With the feeling that they were going to collide with the gate, they effortlessly passed through it, heading towards a large cross that was in the cemetery and he did collide with it with great force. He had a sensation that he was rising but, in fact, he was falling down a dark tunnel and finally landed in a place that seemed to be a dark forest. He was somewhere that he had never had been before, probably some "department of hell."

The guide then told him: "From this point on you will go alone," and left him. After walking a little in that dark place, he spotted a large throne with a really macabre, ten-foot tall, entity sitting on it. Walking in front of the throne, this entity uncrossed his arms, spreading his hands (claws) before him. He understood that should put his hands in the hands of that scary creature. A little afraid, he faltered, but the creature did not move until he gathered enough courage and did what he was there to do: receive power. An enormous heat energized him, indicating that he had plugged in to the powers of that demonic principality.

---

[5]Umbanda is an Afro-Brazilian religion that blends African religions with Catholicism, Spiritism (influenced by, but not limited to, Kardecism) and considerable indigenous lore.

What took place as he was narrating this pact he made was unforgettable. He was viciously attacked, contorting in front of me. Through clenched teeth a strange voice that was not his began speaking threateningly: "Don't tell! Don't tell!" I helped him, telling him to respond and not let it take control of him. Trying to explain to me what he was feeling, he said that something was implanted in his back, like an umbilical cord, as if he had become a hybrid with that entity. It really was a war that was taking place in front of me!

Finally, the secret of his powers was brought to light, in true repentance and repudiation. He repented of his idolatry of mystical powers. We undid the pact made inside of hell during that astral journey, disconnecting him from that terrible entity. We dealt with many other situations and experiences that he had through witchcraft. It was an unforgettable experience. You see, this brother was the leader of an intercession and deliverance ministry, ministering and laying his hands on many people in his church.

• *Inner healing vs. regression*

It is necessary to demystify the concept of inner healing. We can define inner healing as: an attitude of consciously facing, with the presence of God and spiritual maturity, the traumas we have not overcome in the past, interacting with injustices, rejections and their sinful reactions through the principles implicit in the sacrifice of Jesus. In this manner we can continue developing our spiritual life toward holiness and service to the body.

It is important to mention that there is a fine line that separates "inner healing" from "regression." Under no circumstances should we confuse the two. Regression, recognized as a scientific tool by many, uses hypnosis-based resources, spiritualism, parapsychology, etc., which, in fact, are based on straightforward demonic manipulation disguised as "mind power" or "scientific methods."

In regression, for example, when a person relaxes their spirit, submitting to the imposition of hands by a "priest with a white coat," the demons enter the person producing the spiritual experiences, some based on real events that happened to the person and others complete lies, that in the end will accentuate the existing trauma or make the person believe in nonexistent traumas. Satan is the father of lies, the articulator of all deception.

To illustrate, a different type of regression can often be observed in the sessions of umbanda, when spiritual entities known as "Cosme and Damian," "Erê," and "Exus Mirins" take possession of the medium's body. Adults, strangely, begin to behave as if they were children. In fact, these entities perform the spiritual task of arresting adults in childhood traumas.

A few years ago I was approached by a couple that was still dealing with the consequences of unfortunate deliverance counseling at their church. The woman, despite being a believer for quite some time, was ministered to through hypnosis. These ministers, although they seemed sincere, were immature and misinformed as counselors.

During a session, after regressing to a state of a 4-year-old, she vividly relived a trauma that had occurred during that phase of her life. Rather than breaking free, she was imprisoned in the situation. Strangely, something disconnected her from her adult reasoning and she went berserk, behaving like a 4-year old child for almost 3 months.

The people responsible for the deliverance did not know what to do and simply hushed up the case, leaving this new problem with the family. When I attended her, I needed to first "deliver her from her deliverance." Only then was I able to address the deeper issues of what she had experienced earlier in life.

Cultural redemption and occultist therapy techniques

This topic is an appendix to this chapter. It is important to discern the manner in which oriental culture syncretizes body therapies with spiritualistic practices involving the invocation of cosmic energies, empowerment, veneration of the ancestors, etc. While there is a wealth of knowledge and practices in eastern customs (breathing exercises, muscle control, stretching, emotional control, etc.), it is all mixed with activities and spiritist principles antagonistic to the Bible. In this way science (alternative) is mixed with false religion.

In new age religions it is believed that the body has an "energy" that circulates throughout the body by means of specific routes called "meridians." This is what they classify as Yin or negative energy and Yang or positive energy. Health would be the result of the balance of these two energies. In contrast, imbalance produces disease. This mechanism of redemption that relies on the balance between good and evil is based on a totally wrong paradigm and is a frontal attack against the absolute truth of salvation in Christ.

For example, acupuncture believes that the stimulation by needles restores the flow of energy. In fact, this vital energy points to an interaction between the human spirit and evil spirits and can be variously called aura, corporeal energy, breath, serpent power (Kundalini), chi, etc.

It is necessary to separate natural things from spiritual things, establishing an understanding of the subtlety of Satan. We should not belittle the scientific aspect of acupuncture, which is based on the stimulation of endorphins in muscle mass by using needles. Because endorphins are analgesic substances, the therapeutic effects are sensitive, even soothing. Thus, acupuncture can be practiced completely disassociated from spiritualistic rituals.

What I want to emphasize is that it would be immature to simply satanize eastern culture and thus eliminate both the good and the evil. This is another way for the enemy to rob us. It is always important to make this distinction between the sin and the sinner, the principle and the contamination. We cannot just throw everything out. In fact, you can separate what is good, healthy and strategic, redeeming them for the sake of the kingdom of God and the welfare of people.

Just as today we have Christian professionals that utilize the benefits of acupuncture, the same can be done in Yoga, Tai-Chi-Chuan, homeopathy, etc., where any kind of "emptying," transcendental meditation, "spiritual empowerment" or "energizing" is invoked. On the contrary, this becomes an opportunity to share the good news of the gospel.

We cannot ignore that demons are always looking to corrupt what can be used constructively—a bad thing, hidden within a good thing. So, in addition to demonizing the resource, demons use them for the purpose of imprisoning their victims in several other types of mistakes.

A weakness of the church is to not understand this demonic intention by agreeing with this demonization, rather than redeeming and utilizing these resources, biblically leveraging them through the principles that govern them.

SYMPTOM 2. Repeated or chronic ailments without clear medical diagnosis, especially if they are hereditary in character

Some theologians make a distinction between illness and disease, suggesting that diseases are related to some dysfunction or biological contamination while evil spirits causes illness. Here is a very important insight: do not spiritualize a disease that has an organic nature nor "medicalize" an illness that is spiritual in nature. It is logical that there could be a combination of disease and illness in the same situation. All these concepts are present in the Bible:

> *"Jesus called his twelve disciples together and gave them authority to cast out evil spirits and to heal every kind of disease and illness" (Mt 10:1).*

Many demonic persecutions or infestations occur through spirits of sickness. In some biblical texts, there is the presence of these three concepts: illness, disease and demons, as well as a description of how they can unite. I purposely chose these texts in the gospel of Luke because he is a doctor, a scientific person, but one who also recognized the spiritual aspect of some diseases:

> *"...along with some women who had been cured of evil spirits and diseases. Among them were Mary Magdalene, from whom he had cast out seven demons" (Lk 8:2).*
> *"...he saw a woman who had been crippled by an evil spirit. She had been bent double for eighteen years and was unable to stand up straight" (Lk 13:11).*

What happens is that when a clear medical diagnosis is unviable, we are left facing various ailments that are strangely evident in people's lives. Some examples would be cases of chronic insomnia, excessive drowsiness, mental blocks, fainting, seizures, some types of epilepsy, weight and pain in the spine, chronic headache, feeling of swelling in the head, twinges in the body, some cases of congenital diseases, etc.

Demonic spirits can take up residence in a person and can take the form of any type of illness, from a simple health disorder to a fatal illness. What characterizes this type of situation is the absence of a medical diagnosis. When you cannot get a scientific diagnosis, the probability is great that you have a spiritual diagnosis. Stated differently, the absence of a scientific diagnosis points to the need for a spiritual diagnosis.

Once, in one of our seminars, we had a case that illustrates well what we are saying. A girl who was desperate had sought us out because of things that were happening in her family. Her older sister had contracted a strange illness that made her waste away. Every medical resource available had been employed in the attempt to discover what was occurring but without success. After becoming a complete invalid confined to bed, she simply died.

Strangely, her sister had said that when she died that the disease would pass to one of her sisters. And that was exactly what had happened. One of her sisters was stricken with the same malady and was at the point of death. The illness was moving from one person to another. Obviously, when something like this happens it is essential to investigate spiritually.

Congenital diseases

One of the recent discoveries of science is that 97% of the genome that was thought to have no function is actually what makes the gene connection with the external environment, connecting or disconnecting it according to the habits and lifestyle of the person.

Previously it was believed that the genetic background influenced more than the habits and way of life of a person's constitution. Today, it has been proven that the environment interferes decisively in the genetic code, promoting changes in the functioning of genes. The genome undergoes many changes, which may be reversible or irreversible in character.

In cancer, modified genes trigger the uncontrolled growth of cells and there are dozens of other genes related to diseases that can be activated or silenced by micro RNAs synthesized in laboratories. (Revista VEJA[6], 22 April 2009).

---

[6] VEJA is a very famous brazilian magazine.

Without wishing to establish a doctrine based on this, several experiments have shown that many congenital diseases can have a spiritual connotation that is tied to spiritual heritage. Here we cross the line between science and faith. This can be verified in that during the deliverance process, while utilizing intercessory confession of generational iniquities, these diseases disappear. This is very characteristic in confronting the occult and familial apostasy: "then the Lord will overwhelm you and your children with indescribable plagues. These plagues will be intense and without relief, making you miserable and unbearably sick" (Dt 28:59).

We cannot discard the possibility of demonic manipulation in human genetics. In fact, if man himself, with his limited human technology, already has access to his genome sequences, imagine the demons. What we can conclude is that genetic modification is not only related to lifestyle (choices, habits, environment), but also with an individual's spiritual condition and family line.

SYMPTOM 3. Chronic sterility

"The glory of Israel will fly away like a bird, for your children will not be born or grow in the womb or even be conceived. Even if you do have children who grow up, I will take them from you. It will be a terrible day when I turn away and leave you alone... But now Israel will bring out her children for slaughter." O Lord, what should I request for your people? I will ask for wombs that don't give birth and breasts that give no milk... The people of Israel are struck down. Their roots are dried up, and they will bear no more fruit. And if they give birth, I will slaughter their beloved children." My God will reject the people of Israel because they will not listen or obey. They will be wanderers, homeless among the nations" (Ho 9:11-17).

This text reflects the relentless infertility of the people of God as a symptom of a stubborn apostasy. The mother or the uterus and breasts also biblically symbolize the potential to generate and sustain not only children, but also relationships, projects, ministries, plans, etc. Fertility is a natural consequence of healthy living, but chronic sterility denounces disorder, rebellion and spiritual death.

It is very common to deal with people who are dominated by an inability to initiate, and especially to finish, what they start. Equally common are people who are frequent victims of strange interruptions in their lives and these disruptions create chronic frustrations in multiple areas of life. Things do not happen as planned or when they do they are strangely aborted.

I have heard many people saying that everything they touch simply dies, ends or gets lost. In a strangely abnormal manner, objects break or disappear, equipment is ruined, pets die, companies go out of business, friendships are abandoned, churches are divided and split, projects succumb, dreams are aborted, feelings are frustrated, marriages destroyed, etc. Obviously this kind of framework describes a symptom of a curse and deserves deliverance counseling.

We can list even more symptoms that demonstrate this sort of spiritual attack: tendency to have involuntary abortions or having experienced multiple spontaneous abortions; chronic and abnormal menstrual problems; loss of uterus and breasts; spiritual, emotional, mental and professional sterility, etc. In short, nothing thrives.

SYMPTOM 4. A framework of family breakup

The family sphere is one of the main fields that demonstrate the existence of demonic infiltration. Much of the enemy's effort boils down to destroying the family. Family fragmentation leaves the individual unprotected and compromises the family's commitment to develop. This creates a situation that becomes chronic and leads to the family's early destruction.

One of the main symptoms of a curse in a society is the loss of family ties. Examples are when a person does not know who their father is, or does not know if a child is theirs or not, or who is in fact the husband or the wife, etc. The absence of these bonds typically mutilates the identity of a person.

Some important things to consider, from the family point of view, is that a curse is in operation when you observe:

– A high percentage of adultery, conjugal separation and divorce in the family history.

– Hatred and family disruption on a grand scale. Brothers who hate their siblings or relatives; parents who do not talk with children for several years or children who completely cut their relationship with parents; chronic situations of violence, strife and even murder within the proper family.

– A family history of role reversal between husband and wife. I once heard the outburst of a woman who said that in her family, which was composed of four sisters, all the women married "wimps." Each of them had to support their husbands and do all the "work" at home.

All of these things are significant because they show a picture of spiritual failure that needs to be confronted in a priestly manner.

SYMPTOM 5. Continuous economic failure, especially when income seem to be sufficient

In the financial arena, the issue is not how much a person earns but the ability of the income to meet existing needs. It is common to see people making more than enough to pay their expenses but by the middle of the month they are running in the red. In contrast, there are others who barely earn enough to cover their expenses but by the end of the month they still have money left over.

The point is sufficiency and peace, not money. An important question that should be examined is how a person relates to money. Money is important but it cannot be supreme. It cannot dictate what we do, or do not do, in life. Our financial life needs to be governed by faith. The righteous will live by faith, not by salary (money). When money ceases to be the servant and becomes the boss, one's spiritual life is out of balance. Jesus made it clear: we cannot serve God and Mammon (riches). Jesus identified the love of money with the presence of Mammon, a very versatile demonic entity, who is present in all areas of human life.

Concerning this financial question, some important things to be considered as symptoms of spiritual attack are:

– Frequent thefts and losses.

– Constant debts, exaggerated consumerism, financial incontinence (diarrhea of the wallet). Enormous and unnecessary expenses that have no explanation or logic; an uncontrollable compulsion to spend, all point to demonic exploitation.

– Miserliness and greed. Paralyzing fear of being without money.

– Cases of bankruptcy and family financial ruin. Parents and grandparents who were rich and simply lost everything, etc.

Financial Education

It is important to understand that a major cause of economic problems is poor financial education. Intelligence is linked to planning. Planning is using your intelligence to your advantage. If you spend less than you earn you will enrich yourself. If you spend more than you earn you will impoverish yourself. It is simple and accurate mathematics. The lack of planning in spending can cause financial ruin.

Additionally, failing to establish the right priorities can be fatal. In first place should be your debts and obligations. Second come your necessities such as food, gasoline, etc. Finally, if funds (and planning) permit, you can address your desires or "wants." "Wants" are expensive and operate at a different level. The Bible says that God will gloriously supply all of our "needs," not all of our "wants." If you put your desires before your needs, you will have serious problems.

Another area of financial rubbish is the culture of credit. If you purchase something on credit, you will pay twice its worth by the time you are finished. If you save money to buy it with cash, you have bargaining power and will pay less that what it is worth. The difference between paying cash and buying on credit can be almost three times the value of the product. It is not a sin to save money in order to achieve a goal. This is actually intelligent.

So if you are financially ignorant, do not blame the devil. You are your own devil!

SYMPTOM 6. Chronic situation of sudden losses, accidents and frequent surgeries

We are not talking about simple accidents such as backing the car into the garage door. You cannot say this is a demonic attack. It is nothing more than incompetence or inattention. I am talking about repeated serious accidents and situations involving strangers, sometimes inexplicable.

Some people are walking disasters. They are continually the victims of serious, dangerous accidents. The accidents come one after another, as if something were insistently trying to destroy them in every way possible. The person suffers automobile accidents, accidents at work, at home, they are involved in confusion and strife, suffering serious injuries which are sometimes even fatal. This merits an investigation.

Another aspect of this symptom is frequent surgeries. Anyone is subject to having some type of surgery; however, when this becomes frequent, it is necessary to look at the person's involvement with the occult, especially spiritualism (Kardecism). I once had a case in which the person underwent seven surgeries in one year. He had been a "patient" of "Dr. Fritz"[7] for years. After his conversion, in addition to bringing constant illnesses to his family, the entity had been feeding on his blood spilled in the frequent surgeries.

SYMPTOM 7. Chronic failure associated with a history of suicides in the family

Every time someone tries to kill himself, he becomes even more hostage to the spirits of death and to the deep feelings of failure regarding the reason he wished to take his own life. Suicide usually establishes a legacy of depression, failure and bankrupts one's lineage.

SYMPTOM 8. Unrestrained anger associated with a history of homicide and crime in the family

Murder invokes a spirit of persecution and imprisonment. It produces a spiritual and social debt that transforms the individual into a prisoner or fugitive. The person feels persecuted and is often in serious danger and receives death threats. Each murder is a blood pact with the spirit of death: *"The victim's nearest relative is responsible for putting the murderer to death. When they meet, the avenger must put the murderer to death"* (Nu 35:19).

The spirit of death begins to influence or manifest itself in a person through episodes of unrestrained wrath, irrational hatred characterized by a desire to kill, thereby imposing on him an increas-

---

[7]Dr. Fritz was a hypothetical German surgeon whose spirit has allegedly been channeled by several Brazilian psychic surgeons, starting with Ze Arigó in the 1950s and continuing up to the present.

ing criminal tendency: *"A murderer's tormented conscience will drive him into the grave. Don't protect him!" (Pr 28:17)*.

The consequences of a murder may also become ruthless in the family and progeny of the criminal. When Joab, chief of the army of Israel, in an unjust act of revenge, coldly murdered Abner, who had just befriend David, David himself mentioned the curse that was now in force:

> *"I vow by the Lord that I and my kingdom are forever innocent of this crime against Abner son of Ner. Joab and his family are the guilty ones. May the family of Joab be cursed in every generation with a man who has open sores or leprosy or who walks on crutches or dies by the sword or begs for food!" (2 Sm 3:28-29)*

Despite their families not having any direct responsibility, they would suffer consequences. David spiritually interpreted the situation, noting that many descendants of Joab would suffer venereal disease, leprosy, crippling ailments, death by murder and poverty. Joab would have the misfortune of witnessing the consequences of his crime on its own family and descendants.

SYMPTOM 9. Insanity and chronic or cyclic mental breakdowns

The framework of a psycho-emotional disorder is typically multifaceted. Various aspects that are often in opposition to each other are superimposed on the individual. The result is an extremely challenging situation that can lead to psycho-emotional bankruptcy. This can bring about hospitalization, depression, multiple personalities, episodes of madness, chronic sadness, loneliness, deep neuroses, phobias, panic, nervous breakdown, etc.

However, these disturbances are normally just the tip of the iceberg. Emotional disorders such as depression are just the symptom of that which has been dying in the person for a long time. This is the direct and indirect result of systematically developing a lifestyle that attacks one's very nature and identity.

It is important to mention that many psycho-emotional breakdowns result from several factors. We must assess the situation from various perspectives: organic, emotional, nutritional, genetic, environmental, etc. We cannot ignore the reality that virtually every type of psycho-emotional breakdown has a spiritual component that cannot be ignored. It is a process that has been years, even decades, in the making. It is not a simple matter to reverse such situations.

It is not logical to think that in the matter of several hours or days you can dismantle something that has taken so long to construct. As

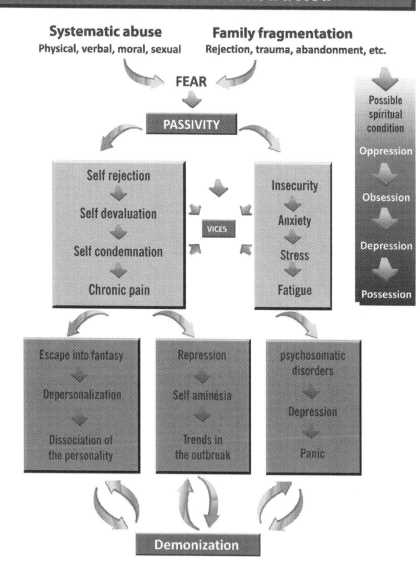

illustrated in the diagram, fear and passivity form the primary battle that must be fought. Reeducation on how to overcome abuse and trauma is necessary.

SYMPTOM 10. Periods of childhood memory that have been erased and a tendency to lose control ("freakout")

This is a more intense version of the previous symptom. A person who has suffered abuse, tried to escape it and failed, ends up erasing or deleting that period of trauma from his memory. Prolonged sexual abuse by one's father (incest) is commonly the catalyst. The suffering is "overcome" by activating a defense mechanism based on self-amnesia (see diagram). The person simply "escapes" this horrible situation by sweeping all the shame and pain under the rug of the soul.

It is common for a person who is trying to deal with such a situation to lose control or "freak out," i.e., he prefers to lose emotional control and nullify the memory than to have to face the torment of his suffering again. In fact, the loss of emotional control is an escape mechanism that is so explosive and intense that it can last for hours and even days. This escape hatch becomes an entryway through which evil spirits can take advantage of the situation. It is a place where the psycho-emotional is mixed with the spiritual.

Counseling that helps the individual to believe that he can, and must, confront this wounded memory through the direction and empowerment of God is the key to the healing of the wound. Often the fear of facing the situation is even more harmful than the situation itself, creating a true spiritual prison for the person. Psychiatric hospitals are full of people who are inappropriately medicated in an unsuccessful attempt to diminish, not remove, that very fear.

I remember a girl I counseled. She related that for years she had told herself she needed to forget something that had happened in her past. Over the years, she had actually succeeded in completely forgetting it. Now she was trying to develop her spiritual life and she knew she needed to face the situation; however, the problem was that no matter how hard she tried, she could not remember what she had forgotten. It was as a lock without a key.

After a time of prayer together, she began to recover her memory, experiencing the terrible trauma of sexual abuse inflicted on her by her father. It was a surgical deliverance, very painful, but effective. Finally, she was able to forgive her father and deal with all the passivity and sexual contamination that she had contracted. She was now able to enjoy the peace that we have in Christ.

An important observation here is that in these situations it is very common for an immature counselor to commit spiritual abuse while attempting to force a solution. Imposing a solution is the exact opposite of counseling. The door is always opened from the inside out, i.e., with the full consent of the person. You encourage the person to redeem the repressed memory and face their pain; however, if the person refuses, you should not insist on going forward.

SYMPTOM 11. Familial transference of behaviors and vices

Familial transference is the clear perception that the identical problem is migrating from one person to another within the family circle. One person will begin to improve in the particular behavior and simultaneously another will begin to develop it. This is the footprint of spirit transference. It can show up in various forms: consumerism, alcoholism, diseases, hypochondria, depression, etc.

> "When an evil spirit leaves a person, it goes into the desert, seeking rest but finding none. Then it says, 'I will return to the person I came from.' So it returns and finds its former home empty, swept, and in order. Then the spirit finds seven other spirits more evil than itself, and they all enter the person and live there. And so that person is worse off than before. That will be the experience of this evil generation." (Mt 12:43-45)

While this text may have a connotation linked to apostasy, it also reveals another interesting spiritual occurrence: the unclean spirit leaves the man and returns to the house. This word house literally refers to the generation of this person – proof of the principle of spirit transference. Obviously these spirits will be transferred to someone who is spiritually vulnerable to their leading.

For example, when a father dies and his wife or one of his children assumes the same negative behavior, there has been a transference of this spirit to another branch of the family tree. This would be a case for deliverance.

SYMPTOM 12. A family profile of chronic, premature deaths, widowhood and death of children

This symptom is present when strange deaths happen repeatedly in the family, e.g., all the men die at the same age; the majority of women die of cancer; all the women become widows prematurely; all the women abort their first child; all firstborn children die young and violently.

This was the pattern of the curse on Eli's house. Eli, in the exercise of his priestly role, had not corrected or punished the ministerial abuses and practice of his children. As a result, he opened a door of destruction and premature death for their successive generations:

> *"Those who survive will live in sadness and grief, and their children will die a violent death. And to prove that what I have said will come true, I will cause your two sons, Hophni and Phinehas, to die on the same day!" (1 Sm 2:33-34)*

SYMPTOM 13. Hereditary sinful behavior: prostitution, divorce, addiction, theft, bastard children, etc.

This symptom becomes obvious when examining a family tree through the previous three to four generations and you discover a high percentage of its members having recurring issues with the same problems; e.g., you find that 90% of the men are alcoholics, 100% of the women are single mothers, 100% of the men are adulterers, 90% of marriages end in divorce, etc.

You do not need to be a spiritual counseling expert to discern that there is a proverbial skunk in the woodpile that has made itself at home in someone's lineage. The accumulated sinful behavior only intensifies the situation and this accelerates the situation's descent into total disaster and collapse.

SYMPTOM 14. Abnormal sexual problems and deviations

Defining marriage

Before we talk about sexual problems, it is essential to define marriage. The essence of marriage and the family is the covenant, i.e., a commitment for the rest of one's life based on loyalty, trust and respect. Four blessings related to the spheres of authority established by God act as spiritual foundations that define the success of marriage:

- The *parents blessing* (family). In the Bible, it is easy to observe that the main institution responsible for marriage is the proper family of the person. Marriages in biblical times were realized through the approval of the parents, at home. In Genesis the Bible shows this linking between marriage and parents: "This explains why a man leaves his father and mother and is joined to his wife, and the two are united into one." (Gn 2:24). The wedding can be summarized as emancipation – the parents give the children authorization to leave them, in honor, assuming a new alliance before God that stands until death separates them.
- The *sacerdotal blessing* (church). The counsel of the leaders and shepherds of a church is essential to confirm such an important step as marriage. Any warning of potential problems or relational adjustments must be taken seriously.
- The *judicial blessing* (government). It is part of our civil and biblical duty to submit to the authorities instituted by God. This brings a legal protection. Failure to establish marriage that is recognized by the state and simply cohabitating creates an illegitimate spiritual situation in marriage.
- The *sexual blessing* (alliance) is established by purity and marital fidelity. Sexual intimacy sanctions and renews the blood covenant between the couple, building the spiritual condition of one flesh, one soul, the affinity of marriage: "...For the Scriptures say, 'The two are united into one.'"(1 Co 6:16). Normally, when the sexual life inside a marriage stops, it is a signal that the marriage is seriously damaged, hurting and in danger. Marriage without sex is not marriage. Contamination issues related to the couples' sex life need to be resolved.

Sexual intimacy in marriage

People are always in conflict about this issue. What can and cannot be done within the confines of conjugal intimacy? Is oral sex a sin? How about anal sex? It is vital to address this issue in a book like this; we have had to counsel many couples that have had to deal with false guilt because of these questions and this always results in serious frustrations.

Another factor here is spiritual abuse that is related to counseling. When any Christian counselor begins to dictate how the sexual intimacy of a couple should occur, he is crossing a dangerous line and committing spiritual abuse. On these issues, it is best to let the Bible speak.

The first relevant consideration is that both oral and anal sex are strongly prohibited in the Bible, but it is always related to the context of homosexuality. For example, when you study the first chapter of the letter of Paul to the Romans, you will realize that the implicit context is not marriage or marital life, but homosexuality and every perversion that is the result of people explicitly denying God and falling into what he calls "unnatural," "shameful" and "burning with lust:"

"That is why God abandoned them to their shameful desires. Even the women turned against the natural way to have sex and instead indulged in sex with each other. And the men, instead of having normal sexual relations with women, burned with lust for each other. Men did shameful things with other men, and as a result of this sin, they suffered within themselves the penalty they deserved." (Rm 1:26-27)

This text cannot be associated with marriage; when the Bible speaks about sodomy, it is important to understand that it is decontextualized from marriage. The concept of sodomy does have its origin in the Bible. Its history is linked to homosexuality found in the story of the inhabitants of Sodom. They wanted to sexually brutalize the men who were staying with Lot and he offered them his daughters in their place. They rejected his offer, preferring to have sex with his male visitors. Though others may want to argue differently, the concept of sodomy is not linked to marriage in the Bible.

Basically, in relation to this aspect of sex, the Bible lays down two fundamental conditions:

• *The first condition is marriage*

Any type of sexual intimacy outside of marriage is sinful and certainly will bring destructive spiritual and social consequences. The Bible is full of innumerable restrictions and prohibitions about sex outside of marriage. In the context of marriage, on the other hand, you will find no biblical references that regulate or restrict what a couple can or cannot do in their sexual intimacy. It simply does not exist! Quite to the contrary, if you study Song of Solomon you will be surprised to discover the importance of eroticism and sexual liberty within marriage.

Marital sex must be viewed as a gift from God to be enjoyed with all of its pleasures. It is important that we break the sophisms that try to imply marital sex is dirty, shameful or indecent. There is absolutely no tolerance for such a stance in a marriage. Conversely, when barriers, constraints or blockades exist in the sexual life of a couple, it is quite probable that a demonic infiltration exists and is enabled by religious or sexual abuses. All biblical restriction in relation to sex is in the context of extramarital activity.

• *The second condition, which depends on the first, is agreement*

He who loves, respects. When there is no respect or approval, there will be violence. Where there is violence, there will be suffering. Pleasure without respect does not exist. If there is agreement, there are no biblical rules or restrictions that govern sexual intimacy within marriage.

Truthfully, Paul's only restriction is related to sexual abstinence (1 Co 7:5), and the couple must commonly agree. Such an agreement being made, it is not to be for a long period of time and the reason for it is consecration and prayer. Unfortunately, for reasons primarily involving displacement due to work, some couples abstain from sexual intimacy for an overly long time. This functions as an invitation for adultery; as Paul warns: *"so that Satan won't be able to tempt you."*

Sex involves a person's whole body. The pleasure the couple enjoys comes from God and our very human anatomy confirms it. This is fundamental to the life of mature people (married) – they have to deal with an incredible amount of tension and responsibility in their day to day lives and sex is highly relaxing (de-stressing). The sexual union refines the intimacy of the couple emotionally and spiritually.

Therefore, since there is agreement, there are no biblical rules or restrictions for sex inside of marriage. Paul endorses by saying: *"The wife gives authority over her body to her husband, and the husband gives authority over his body to his wife." (1 Co 7:4).*

Obviously, this text explains that sex is connected to the body and not just part of it. This involves the mind, all the senses (sight, hearing, taste, touch and smell) as well as all the skin (not part of it), the nervous, glandular and hormonal systems, etc. Sex encompasses the entire body.

Look, it was God who created human anatomy this way, not the devil! It is logical that if one spouse does not feel comfortable with some form of sexual activity, it must be respected. He who loves, respects. However, in that activity where both parties are stimulated and mutually fulfilled, there is no sin or condemnation. This type of taboo must be eliminated. It is this type of religiosity that can destroy a marriage.

Caveats to consider

• In regards to anal sex, we should consider Paul's advice:

You say, "I am allowed to do anything"—but not everything is good for you. And even though "I am allowed to do anything," I must not become a slave to anything. You say, "Food was made for the stomach, and the stomach for food." (This is true, though someday God will do away with both of them.) But you can't say that our bodies were made for sexual immorality. They were made for the Lord, and the Lord cares about our bodies. (1 Co 6:12-13)

Despite the context of this text being "prostitution" and not "marital sex" and we do not find any biblical prohibition against anal sex associated with marital life, I think that even thought it may be "allowed" and there may be an existing consensus between the couple, it is not appropriate for a number of reasons of organic, physiological, emotional, hygienic nature. This is advice (not a rule) that I give to those who ask me about this.

• Also, because of past involvements and contaminations of a couple with sexual perversion, such as a woman who sought me out for help who came from a homosexual past and can only derive sexual pleasure from verbal sex now that she is married, the Holy Spirit can convince them that they should not be involved in this form of sex. But, this has to come from a personal conviction by the Holy Spirit in their lives and not a rule imposed on them by a counselor.

It is an error to want to impose doctrine on conjugal intimacy. Not even the Bible does this. If the Bible does not establish sexual rules for marriage, I do not think that we should want to act wiser than God. Therefore, what we have here, without criticizing the zeal of the people who act this way, is that they take a text out of context, force an interpretation under the pretense of holiness and unknowingly end up abusing the conjugal intimacy of others.

These sexual restrictions inside of marriage can sound spiritual, but they are not. It interferes with the intimacy of people by creating a biblical mandate where none exists. This type of sophism simply strengthens the religious spirit and deprives the couple of their freedom and responsibility that has been granted by God Himself. It is worthwhile to note another of Paul's counsel: *"You may believe there's nothing wrong with what you are doing, but keep it between yourself and God. Blessed are those who don't feel guilty for doing something they have decided is right."* (Rm 14:22).

Attraction and intention

To clarify intersexual relations it is relevant to make a distinction between these two concepts: attraction and intention. There is a distance between attraction and sexual intention. This is the same distance that exists between hunger and greediness, thirst and drunkenness, sleep and laziness, zeal and jealousy, etc. They are different things and should not be confused.

Attraction and intention are at the base of temptation and sin respectively. Attraction corresponds to temptation, as does intention to sin. Attraction and temptation are involuntary. Intention and sin, however, imply an inner decision being made and therefore involves responsibility.

All temptation can be defeated and all sin can be prevented. To defeat temptation is a question of speed. The great key in dealing with temptation is to not entertain it. The faster we say "No!" the easier it is to defeat it.

If we can understand this distance between temptation and sin, it is possible to conclude that we sin less than we think we do. The greater danger is to confuse temptation with sin; that will cause us to equivocally declare when tempted: "I sinned in my thoughts!" This can become a false excuse: "Since I sinned in thought, I might as well complete the act!" This is a prescription for disaster!

It is essential to understand that the intersexual attraction is something instinctive, natural, biological and hormonal. All normal human beings, in relation to the opposite sex, are subject to physical attraction. We need to work with the intention. That is, attraction is basically hormonal, while intention is basically moral. We do not have to castrate sexual desire, but we do have to dominate it.

Sin is, strictly speaking, a question of intention and not attraction. Sexual desire in itself does not have to be declawed. To do so would be to establish a bondage that attacks our proper nature. Attraction without illicit intention has no sinful connotation. I think it is important to clarify this. Many people carry a terrible weight of condemnation for the simple fact that they feel sexually attracted to someone and the reality is that they are merely normal.

An acquaintance of mine that took his spiritual life very seriously came to me and confessed: "Pastor, I am a terrible sinner!" I was concerned and asked him what had happened? He answered: "Sometimes I find myself sexually attracted to other women!" (It is worth noting that he lives in a city where the women are terribly provocative). Then I questioned him if when this had occurred if he had arrived at the conclusion that he would pursue a relationship with them if the opportunity were to arise. His response: "Never! I am faithful to my family!" Upon explaining to him that what was happening was occurring because he was normal, his reaction was as if a ton of false conviction lifted off his shoulders. That was deliverance!

Sexual desire is a natural faculty in the life of any human being. This is part of one's own body chemistry. No one is immune to sexual attraction. However, it is important to realize that the appetite and sexual attraction can suffer severe imbalances and that this is an indication of an infiltration of a spiritual character.

Lets now address the latent symptoms that are proof of a spiritual attack in the sexual arena:

SYMPTOM A. Homosexual tendency

Tendencies towards homosexuality are strong sexual attractions for people of the same sex with no attraction for the opposite sex. Intersexual attraction is part of human nature; however, homosexual attraction indicates non-human infiltration by a spirit of sexual perversion. Homosexuality can also develop through other misrepresentations as:

- *Transexualism:* The individual does not accept his sex and desires to change it. Since infancy the person has experienced homosexual attacks so intense that he feels he is sexually inadequate. This is something highly demonic. This is not merely flesh and blood or hormones. The person is convinced that he was born as the wrong sex. He often hates God and is a spiritual rebel. This seed of perversion contaminates other areas of life.

- *Transvestism:* Intense and compulsory desire to dress in the clothes of the opposite sex. This type of spiritual imprisonment demonstrates a malignant conflict occurring in the identity. This is an extreme symptom of homosexual attack that not only shows the necessity of deliverance, but of a process of re-education of the identity.

SYMPTOM B. Disordered sexual desire

There are two extremes in relation to sexual desire: sexual neurosis and impotence without clear medical diagnosis.

• *Sexual neurosis*
Sexual neurosis is based on a huge, uncontrollable sexual appetite. Once a missionary came to me asking for help. He summarized his problem saying he masturbated about ten times a day. He realized that he had become a compulsive sex maniac.

Today we help organizations such as Sex Addicts Anonymous that have many Christians in attendance. They are obviously people who need help. It is common to hear stories of people having fifteen sexual encounters (without the help of Viagra) in a single night … it is logical that these people are empowered by spirits of sexual perversion and they certainly need deliverance.

• Impotence and frigidity
The other extreme is the lack of sexual, i.e., cases of marital or sexual impotence that have no clear any medical diagnosis.

Female frigidity
In relation to female frigidity, what we typically find is:

– *Hidden adultery*. Incredibly, in most cases, adultery opens the door of frigidity and even sexual aversion in marriage.

– *Sexual abuse in childhood*. Women traumatized by sexual abuse develop a demonic stronghold that is sexual in character. It is a dormant weapon that is activated after the wedding and produces a kind of "chastity belt." This becomes a prison that ends up destroying the couple's sex life, leaving it susceptible to adultery and divorce. It is something intensely evil.

Male impotence
– *Witchcraft*. It is amazing how many cases of marital impotence are associated with a past not cleansed of sexual immorality and witchcraft.

In one of our seminars, a psychologist volunteered for a demonstration of how spiritual counseling works. Her biggest dilemma was that it had been six years since she had engaged in sexual relations with her husband. This had created a terrible frustration that was strongly influencing various aspects of her life. Even having accepted the gospel three years prior, the situation simply had not changed.

I asked if she suspected that there had been something specific that had produced this situation. My question caused the reason of her problem to surface. Her husband had never been faithful to her since the beginning of her marriage. This had created a growing bitterness and rebellion. Everyone in her family knew what was happening and her mother, who had a long history of utilizing the occult, suggested that she look up someone adept in spiritism that could help her "fix" her situation.

Even though she did not really believe in these things, she ended up going to see someone. The ritual took place in a totally dark room. The "practitioner" handed her a cylindrically shaped object and told her that she should bite it as hard as she could until he told her to stop. She related that she had the sensation that the man was masturbating while reciting a series of prayers and spells.

After that session, her husband never again betrayed her, but he also never had sex with her again. In fact, he had become supernaturally impotent. I asked her if she had ever told her husband about her revenge. Though remorseful, she replied that she had never had the courage to do so. We prayed, asking for God's forgiveness and canceled the ritual where the husband's sexual organ had been spiritually "mutilated."

I suggested then that she confront the situation, not just forgiving her husband of his betrayals, but also asking forgiveness from him for the bitterness and revenge that had been offered through this macabre ritual. She went home resolute to do so. A few days later she appeared with a broad smile. Incredibly, she and her husband had had a honeymoon after six years of sexual abstinence.

– *Pornography*. There is a demonic connection between pornography and marital impotence. This may seem to be contradictory seeing how pornography is a sexual stimulant, but it is a fact. There is a spiritual logic in this reasoning. We know that a man is sexually aroused by what he sees. His hormones are activated by his physical sense of seeing. In fact, for most men, visual sex gives more pleasure that the actual act itself.

Satan's primary target with pornography is to attack the figure of the husband and father. Due to difficulties in the conjugal sexual relationship, and pornography's ease of access, the man can easily take refuge in it. He ends up becoming totally absorbed in it and begins to exchange sex with his wife for sex by porn, spending hours every day immersed in pornography.

In many cases, what we have seen is that the more one engages in porn, the more he will lose sexual interest in his wife. His sexual desire begins to migrate from inside to outside of marriage. Sexual intimacy in marriage malignantly loses grace and dies.

SYMPTOM C. Sexual Sorcery

There are many people who engage in the occult in search of sexual favors. The result is that they begin to be accompanied by spirits of seduction. They receive a supernatural ability of seduction and attraction that is simultaneously emotional and sexual. These malignant influences function as a sexual pheromone.

Even after having accepted the gospel and attending a church, some people continue to carry a spirit of sensuality and emotional seduction. They emotionally pursue someone and when their "prey" falls in love with them, they feel disgust for them and reject their now smitten former target. Barely out of that relationship, they already move to another. So it goes, collecting broken hearts and hurt feelings. In other cases, after falling in love and sexually engaging with spiritually vulnerable people, they are assaulted by a terrible loathing for their prey. These episodes of passion, seduction, fornication and repulsion repeat itself with several people, in different churches, producing enormous emotional and spiritual damage.

SYMPTOM D. Sexolatry, pornography and masturbation

This is the direction taken by a person with a mind addicted to sexual fantasies. It is essential to establish a limit for these fantasies. The mind is the main spiritual battlefield and it is there that we decide if we will control our desires and feelings or if they will spiritually control us.

Today we are experiencing an eroticized culture. Sex is increasingly becoming an idol for us. The brain is the primary sexual organ of the human being and there is no limit to the sexual fantasies it can create. These fantasies can evolve into neuroses, which in turn become powerful demonic connections that imprison us. These chains are destroying the spiritual, ministerial, marital and family life of many people.

SYMPTOM E. Constant erotic dreams and sexual relations with spirits

This is quite strange, but is increasingly present in spiritual counseling. People who have been willing to reveal their experiences have described this type of spiritual disturbance, being constantly harassed sexually by demonic spirits. It is something literally supernatural and oppressive. In practice, we can unravel three situations that may be present in this symptom:

— *Legacy of sexual perversion in the family* (homosexuality, incest, etc.). Depending on the instances, the generational immorality can open a door of oppression, persecution, and obsession and even create this terrible situation where the person begins to be sexually approached by demonic spirits.

— *Bestiality*. Bestiality is spiritually a blood pact, a marriage with demonic spirits of sexual perversion. The person is vulnerable to this type of sexual approach.

— *Occult wedding* (marriage or sexual relationship in occultism). Some sex practiced ritualistically in witchcraft, especially with people who occupy priestly positions, constitutes a marriage between the person and the entity represented by this priest.

Once, a lady approached me and though she was already married and taking a preparatory course to develop an international missionary project, she was living this nightmare. I asked her when this began and the story she told me unlocked the nature and the true cause of the problem.

She came from a home deeply involved in the occult. Her mother was actually a priestess in the occult religion that she practiced. There was also an occult priest who channeled the spirit of their temple, who, according to him, was a demonic entity of Lucifer.[8] Shortly before completing her sixteenth birthday, her mother gave her a message from the priest, which said she needed to perform an important ritual and offering on her birthday.

In obedience to her mother, she simply went. In the middle of her testimony, she said: "until today, I don't know if my mother knew what would happen to me there." It really was tragic. She was taken to a reserved place where she was alone with this man who was the priest of the temple. She described how visible the demonic presence was when it physically entered the priest. Inexplicably, almost without reaction, the spirit who was incorporated in the priest sexually deflowered her. Only later did she discover

---

[8] Exú-lúcifer.

that the "offering" that the entity wanted was the virginity of a 16-year old girl.

After this event she began to experience nightly spiritual sexual advances. She would invisibly feel this entity poking her body and coming to her bed. In fact, what had happened in the ritual was a wedding. Her mother had given her in marriage to the demonic entity of Lucifer and now the demon was coming to his conjugal bed, putting her into position for his rightful intimacy with her.

Even though she had accepted the gospel and had married, this demonic exploitation continued, albeit more mildly. It is logical that this type of situation is evidence of a spiritual attack and it demands deliverance counseling.

SYMPTOM F. Pedophilia

Pedophilia is a sexual attraction for children. Typically, people abused in childhood become adult pedophiles. This is the type of connection that can span generations and is something sickening. When an adult begins to have sexual desires for children, there really is something very wrong with him. Certainly there are many spiritual and sexual problems rooted in his personal and family history. The abuses happen more frequently with persons of the same family, but it is worth mentioning that one of the favorite places for pedophiles is the church and in children's and youth ministries.

In the U.S. a report of child abuse[9] is made every 10 seconds, regardless of social class. The aggression is physical, psychological, emotional and moral. Once a person stops seeking help, it is only a matter of time until they are discovered. Many end up in prison.

SYMPTOM G. Exhibitionism

Exhibitionism can be defined as an abnormal desire to view the sexual organs. When a person loses touch with modesty and becomes seduced by the desire to seduce others by displaying his sexual organs, it evidences a strong demonic infiltration.

---

[9]Source: USHHS-ACF, Prevent Child Abuse New York, Children's Defense Fund.

In the fall of man we see that there is a shame that God clothed: *"and the Lord God made clothing from animal skins for Adam and his wife." (Gn 3:21).* Sin made man aware of his nudity and brought shame. The Bible talks a lot about clothes. God wants to handle our shame by dressing us in justice, happiness, holiness, praise, etc. In turn, Satan wants to demoralize us through nudity and indiscretion: *"a beautiful woman who lacks discretion is like a gold ring in a pig's snout." (Pr 11:22).*

Exhibitionism will always incite a desire that will not be satisfied in the correct way. This is the beginning of the demonic fraud. Exhibitionism is mainly an area of temptation for women, since the man is attracted mainly by what he sees. When someone feels the urge to seduce or entice people to desire them through exposing themself, obviously, there is a latent spiritual infiltration.

We could list several perverted sexual practices that need to be confronted and worked with in deliverance. Some of them are unbelievable: Masochism, Sadomasochism, Voyeurism, Coprophagia, Necrophilia, urolagnia, etc.

2

THE MAPPING
PROCESS

Definition

According to our diagram, spiritual mapping corresponds to the distance between the symptoms of a curse and their respective causes. This is the process of establishing a diagnosis. Mapping is built on the ability to bridge the spiritual distance between the presented symptoms of a curse and its sustaining causes through research (interview) and especially God's revelation.

Mapping is the aim of the counseling process and deliverance; it is the means through which we understand the true nature and causes of the problem. It is the process of investigation that unravels the true causes of the symptoms. Failures in this process severely compromise the results of counseling.

The first thing we learned in the field of deliverance is that in order to achieve definitive solutions we must solve the causes, and not the symptoms, of the problem. We need to know how to interpret symptoms from a personal, territorial and systemic perspective. The insight that is gained helps to unveil the true roots of the problem that needs to be addressed.

One of the most important aspects of intercession is spiritual mapping. Insight and perseverance are essential to search, track and map personal family, hereditary and territorial history: wounds, traumas, injustices suffered or practiced, repeated sins, strongholds of the mind, stories of abuse and abandonment, ways of life based on inverted values, broken alliances, prophecies and demonic legacy, relevant crimes, etc.

The power of intelligent confession

Heather Marjorybanks, an experienced YWAM missionary who works with the spiritual mapping of nations, gave the following account:[1]

"During the second world war, 53,000 bombs were needed to hit a desired target. In the Korean War this number dropped to 16,000 bombs. During the Vietnam War this number was reduced to 700. In the Gulf war, absolute precision weapons guaranteed that a single missile could be employed against a single target. Today, we can engage in a "surgical" war with "smart" missiles where each missile has the ability to achieve precisely the target designated."

This same military precision is true in the spiritual reality when the principles of spiritual mapping and cartography are applied. The better a curse or spiritual attack is mapped, the more intelligent, and necessary, confession and intercession become. The results are tangible. Intelligent confession is the most important aspect of intercession. The ability to accurately map the personal, hereditary and territorial blame defines the effectiveness of intercession. Without this objectivity, we become confused and pastorally ineffective when facing a framework of persecution or spiritual imprisonment.

The revelation of God is dynamic. The Lord is always revealing insights and calling to memory both old and new strategies for his church that allow us to always stay one step ahead of the enemy. Spiritual mapping is the element that provides dexterity and skill in spiritual warfare. James calls it the *"prayer of a righteous person"* which has *"great power and produces wonderful results" (Ja 5:16)*. It accurately discerns the "blame" that needs to be intelligently acknowledged.

The success of deliverance depends on the assertiveness of the diagnosis. The mapping process leads us to a spiritual depth with the correct diagnosis. This allows us to make intelligent, objective and enlightening intercessions and confessions with accurate results.

---

[1] Heather Marjoribanks, "Seminário de Mapeamento Espiritual realizado em Curitiba," 2004

– *Interview and research*

A wise interview and an appetite for research are vital to the process of deliverance. Every liberator needs to develop an appetite for the investigative spirit; it is the key to successful deliverance and is part of our priestly ministry.

Studying the office of the priest in the Old Testament, primarily in the book of Leviticus, we can see that the responsibility to investigate is what gives a specific diagnosis, such as in the case of a plague, leprosy, adultery, murder, etc.

The liberator, as an intercessor, needs to develop a profile of a "spiritual researcher." He must follow clues, correctly read the symptoms that are present, ask the right questions and, above all, listen to the Holy Spirit. This enables him to bring everything that is still under the jurisdiction of the prince of darkness into the light. Demons will do anything to prevent certain revelations that support their claim of injustice from coming to light. If the real cause of a curse are ignored or remain hidden, the spiritual attack can continue.

The first principle of counseling is to listen to the person. To discern what is happening, it is necessary to hear. To hear, you need to be an active listener. To do this, it is essential to strip away our autobiography, i.e., our own personal history and experience through which we understand things, and any other type of cultural or religious filter that would color our understanding. We must understand the problem from the person's point of view while using a biblical worldview. Discernment, wisdom and compassion must go together.

– *Revelation*

The essence of revelation is reliance on God: this is the soul of spiritual mapping. Dependence on God is the lever of revelation. What we discover through research and interview can be obtained through a revelation from God. Revelation is more important than information. It goes beyond information and produces a complete understanding of the framework. Information is very helpful, but revelation releases a supernatural intervention by God that not only brings to light what is needed but also defines the question.

This biblical episode perfectly illustrates this concept:

> *There was a famine during David's reign that lasted for three years, so David asked the Lord about it. And the Lord said, "The famine has come because Saul and his family are guilty of murdering the Gibeonites." (2 Sm 21:1)*

A famine (drought) for three consecutive years is something that captures the attention of any city. Obviously by this time David's government had been trying to make sense out of what was happening. It is likely that many details had been raised but nothing helped them change the situation.

David finally decides to consult God. Better late than never. Ignoring science and human experience, he simply listens to what God had to reveal. That divine revelation clearly showed the true source of the problem: *"The famine has come because Saul and his family are guilty of murdering the Gibeonites."*

The family of Saul is denounced as "guilty of murder." The crimes that Saul had committed against the Gibeonites, which also included the breaking of the alliance Joshua made with them, were the reason for the drought. This is a case in point where the power of revelation provides the key to spiritual mapping. How many years would that famine had lingered if not for David's initiative to free the land? How many people, families, churches, towns are suffering and being destroyed due to negligence in this same way?

The dynamics of revelation is the fruit of disciplining our soul to a constant dependence on the Holy Spirit, recognizing that glory belongs to God alone, i.e., worship generates revelation and revelation produces worship. It is simply breathtaking.

In this field it is forbidden to lean on your own understanding. In mapping it is necessary to establish a powerful synergy between research and revelation. Research produces revelation and revelation helps to further research. We must listen to people as well as listen carefully to God. We should listen more and talk less. We have two ears and only one mouth. If you do not hear the person, you probably will not hear God. When we hear the person, we simultaneously create an opportunity for God to speak. At the right moment comes a word of knowledge that reveals everything, increasing the effectiveness of counseling.

These are the two legs of spiritual mapping: research and revelation. Walking with these two legs it is easy to cover the spiritual distance between a real symptom of a curse and causes that sustain it.

Biblical principles of spiritual mapping

The book of Joshua brings an unparalleled wealth of understanding to the principles of deliverance and restoration of the soul. The book of Exodus allegorically emphasizes the experience of salvation, namely, the departure from Egypt. God judged all the deities of Egypt; the Nile River which was worshiped as the source of prosperity, and death which was eerily cultivated through the megalomaniacal pyramids or tombs. Stated differently, the ten principal gods of Egypt were struck down by the ten plagues of Moses. Thus, God delivered Israel from slavery to a new life. It is like a new birth. This is the process of being taken from the world, the power of darkness, and being transported to the kingdom of the Son of His love. Crossing the Red Sea with Moses illustrates the baptism of salvation.

Then came the desert, where God dealt with the mentality of slavery. This points to an internal change of values that matures us so that we can take possession of the promised land. This was a more laborious step where many perished. The crossing of the Jordan, with Joshua, marked this spiritual advancement.

Soon after comes the deliverance of the land. The land is the soul. The conquest of the promised land is nothing more than the gradual surrender of each area of our soul to God. We practice a disciplined lifestyle of renunciation and brokenness when, under the rule of the Spirit, we deal with the areas of control. The strongholds, the giants, the sinful structures that conspire against the kingdom of God are executed, one by one. The Holy Spirit needs to put the soles of your feet on each area of your soul. The big question of conquest lies in our being conquered.

The presence of enemies in Israel has always been associated with the absence of God, and the absence of enemies has always been associated with the presence of God. In Canaan we observe the breadth of the soul – many regions, hills and valleys occupied by enemy structures that need to be conquered, demanding our decision and a posture of brokenness, faith, obedience and perseverance.

Canaan allegorizes the quality of life we enjoy in Christ. The soul is like a land of milk and honey, a land of plenty, but infested with enemies. Canaan is within us. The conquest of abundant living is not immediate. Jesus taught: *"By standing firm, you will win your souls"* *(Lk 21:19); "If any of you wants to be my follower, you must turn from your selfish ways, take up your cross, and follow me." (Mt 16:24).*

We must not confuse the immediate experience of the new birth with the progressive experience of the conversion of the soul. The biblical concepts are different. As explained above, in "the new birth" the spirit is recreated. It is a critical experience, it marks us, it is a large watershed. However, the "the conversion of the soul" is a dynamic process that involves all areas of our life.

In spite of salvation and the change of values that enslaved us in Egypt (life without God), there still exists in the Canaan of our soul spiritual prisons and strongholds that need to be destroyed, kings (areas of selfishness) that need to be overthrown, internal giants (areas of intimidation) that need to be defeated, walls and strongholds (relational and emotional barriers) that have to be knocked down. Much space needs to be conquered and populated in the Canaan of our soul.

The profile of a mapper

We do not have space for a thorough study of the book of Joshua, but I want to at least point out the ministry of the spies, which integrated the importance of the spiritual mapping of the land with the process of the deliverance and conquest of the soul.

> *"Then Joshua secretly sent out two spies from the Israelite camp at Acacia Grove. He instructed them, 'Scout out the land on the other side of the Jordan River, especially around Jericho.' So the two men set out and came to the house of a prostitute named Rahab and stayed there that night." (Js 2:1)*

Dissecting this verse, we can establish not only the importance and the basic concept of spiritual mapping, but also some other important principles that I would like to point out:

1. Priestly Maturity:

Mapmakers have to be people invested with authority and experience. This is not a task for neophytes. Not everyone has the aptitude for this. The first time Moses sent out the twelve spies, he chose a prince from each of the tribes of Israel. They were men of high rank who really should have been mature, experienced in leadership and having a priestly capacity to represent the people. Yet, in the face of intimidation and opposition they faced as they scoped out the land, they reacted with disbelief. Their failure in the mapping of the land cost the nation of Israel a pilgrimage of 38 years in the desert. When you fail in the mapping process, the deliverance process is interrupted.

After this first failure in the mapping process under Moses, Joshua now selects once again from the same group. But this time he only chooses two men, honoring those among the twelve who believed in the deliverance of the land.

2. Spiritual Commissioning: "Joshua ... sent ..."

Mappers need to be sent from God. They must be legitimately authorized and commissioned by the Holy Spirit, as well as under the spiritual coverage of a supporting leadership that accepts this commissioning the mappers have received. This may not appear to be something significant, but this kind of support makes all the difference.

Joshua incorporates the typology of the Holy Spirit. The most important aspect in spiritual mapping is a legitimate dependency and obedience to God. There can be no room for presumption and independence. People who engage in this field need to have an attitude of cooperation with leadership and be legitimately oriented and called by God.

3. Unity, partnership, agreement: "... two spies ..."

The number two is the difference between a person and a church. Two people, gathered in the name of Jesus, bring a tremendous advantage for God to prevail against the gates of hell. In the field of mapping, intercession and deliverance, we must always think in terms of a team context.

Mapping involves interdependence and agreement between the counselor and the counselee to discern truly relevant information. It is essential to cultivate healthy relationships and circumvent anxiety, control, manipulation or any other toxic motivation that would hinder openness. The legitimate authority and capacity to map depends on agreement, interdependence and complementary ministerial gifts.

4. Support, coverage: "... from... Acacia Grove ..."

Acacai Grove (Sittim) was where all the forces of Israel assembled. Mappers need a ministerial rearguard, a "Headquarters," a base of operations. It is essential to be backed by a robust ministerial structure. This is where a fundamental role of the church comes in, promoting advances and progress against the gates of hell through smart shepherding, freeing people and territories that are under demonic bondage.

Mappers cannot be people who are isolated and independent. They must be capable of representing the ministerial environment that commissioned them.

5. Prudence, skill, dexterity: "...secretly ..."

In developing this spiritual expertise in spiritual mapping, we need to develop some traits that are crucial in the lifestyle of a liberator:

• Discretion. Mappers need be good observers, discrete, loyal, dependable people who know how to keep secrets and respect the privacy of others. Gossip is the ministerial suicide of a counselor.
• Free of the lust for recognition. A mapper needs to be a person who has already overcome the barriers of emotional needs, someone who does not need to call attention to himself, who does not try to impress others with his spirituality, exposing themselves to the enemy and undermining the process. Maturity and discreetness will not negotiate ethics.
• Knows how to face the enemy without overvaluing it, fully trusting in the person, character and provision of God.

6. Power of mobility and spiritual observation: "... Scout out the land... "

These are the two main actions of mapping. We can see the concept of spiritual mapping in a simplified and comprehensive manner here: the investigative ability to traverse the territory of soul in emotional, mental, moral and spiritual areas. From this we can establish two basic actions:

– The first verb is to scout. The mapper must have the pastoral ability to traverse all the strongholds of the human soul, sorting it all out through intelligent questions and approaching the person's pains through compassion.

This is what the good Samaritan did for the man who was a victim of thugs: *"Then a despised Samaritan came along, and when he saw the man, he felt compassion for him..." (Lk 10:33).* To be able to help someone who is wounded it is necessary to empathize, to feel the pain of the person.[2] This is the great secret of spiritual mapping. The closer you get to the ruins of one's soul, the more you feel God's heart for him. Compassion generates empathy, empathy generates responsibility. This results in the ability to help and make a difference.

The same example can be observed in Nehemiah as he rode through the ruins of Jerusalem: *"After dark I went out through the Valley Gate, past the Jackal's Well, and over to the Dung Gate to inspect the broken walls and burned gates..." (Ne 2:13).*

Jerusalem means "place of peace." It represents the soul where God's Kingdom is established but is now in captivity. Quietly, dodging the enemies of Jerusalem, Nehemiah was able to see the real situation of the city. The mapper must have moral courage and wisdom to approach the ruins of the soul of people, to get a close look at the landscape. The temple looted and destroyed, the altar overthrown – it is a picture of death, spiritual absence. The city walls were turned into dust, i.e., the soul's spiritual boundaries destroyed and its gates burned, the soul totally unprotected and at the mercy of an enemy invasion.

– The second verb of mapping is to observe, i.e., to take a correct reading of the situation, examine in depth, obtain the information necessary to resolve the situation. Mapmakers need to know how to value relevant details and develop an investigative spirit.

---

[2] The medical definition of empathy is " the action of understanding, being aware of, being sensitive to, and vicariously experiencing the feelings, thoughts, and experience of another of either the past or present without having the feelings, thoughts, and experience fully communicated in an objectively explicit manner." Sympathy is an understanding of a situation but not the vicarious experiencing of it. It is important to note that we have all experienced emotional, spiritual and ethical pain; we can experience the person's pain. If we do not allow ourselves to feel their pain, we have greatly diminished our ability to help them heal their wounds.

7. Identify the external nature of the fortress:
"... around Jericho ..."

This is an amplification of the previous principle. There was a specific target. They were to walk and observe, not only the land, but also Jericho. The basis of any deliverance is dealing with the spiritual strongholds that have been established in the person's soul; these are the areas of self-protection, self-affirmation, compensation, escape and chaos. Jericho is the fortress seen from the outside. You know the direction to take in working with the individual by the behavioral barriers he presents.

This helps us get to the roots of the problem; you must learn to recognize the strongholds the enemy has put in place in a person's soul. Jericho is the perfect typology, the externalization of a spiritual stronghold that has been internally erected in a person's life. Strongholds are often built by thoughts and feelings contrary to God's wisdom and enslave us through sectarian behavior.

In the New Testament, when Paul talks about the strongholds of the mind, he literally means "a prison formed by enemy thoughts of divine wisdom, areas where the person, even knowing that he is practicing something contrary to the will of God, has lost hope of being able to reverse the situation." These are the main areas that need to be mapped and worked on in deliverance.

8. Penetrate the stronghold:
"...came to the house ... and stayed there."

Here we have a deepening of the process. Entering the house signifies delving into the family history, developing a systemic understanding of what has occurred. We are a product of our family history.

In all of Jericho there was only one house that had the attention of the spies. The owner of the house was a woman Peter described as a "fragile vase," which from our perspective here represents the vulnerable aspect that a stronghold establishes in a person's life.

This demonstrates that the bigger the external stronghold, the greater the internal fragility. Just like the spies, it is the route that the spiritual mapper must follow, entering the external stronghold (problem) in order to get the wounded area (Rahab's house).

Knock on the right doors. With his permission, get to the place where the person is vulnerable, that place where he has lived under condemnation, concealment and disloyalty. Identify those specific areas that will provide significant information about the person's real spiritual situation.

9. Identify the inner nature of the stronghold: "...a prostitute named Rahab."

The spies gained personal access to Rahab; they did not simply go to her house, they slept there. The mapper must have access to things that are done in darkness. They must gain the permission of the person to enter places where the person did not want anyone to go. It is necessary to bring light to those areas that are a reservoir of emotional pain and shame.

The mapper, bringing the grace of God, penetrates the soul's brothel. He enters those areas where the person has prostituted himself, sold himself, short changed himself, degraded himself — these are areas of deep pain and shame. It is in this place that he has constructed prisons of guilt and hatred of himself.

The base of the stronghold is the wound, the shame, the guilt. It is necessary to carry the deliverance to these fragile areas where the person has suffered moral, spiritual, physical and/or sexual abuse, where his soul and identity have been crippled. Every stronghold has its origin in injury or wounds. Injury establishes deformed feelings and thoughts that conspire against the freedom of the soul.

Despite the stigma that the word prostitute carries, this person has a name — Rahab — and an identity that needs to be rescued and redeemed. Each deliverance is personal. The mapper must have the ability to penetrate the stronghold and get the intimate information that will be crucial for a thorough and definitive liberation.

10. Plunder the fortress:

"For we have heard how the Lord made a dry path for you through the Red Sea when you left Egypt. And we know what you did to Sihon and Og, the two Amorite kings east of the Jordan River, whose people you completely destroyed. No wonder our hearts have melted in fear! No one has the

courage to fight after hearing such things. For the Lord your God is the supreme God of the heavens above and the earth below. Now swear to me by the Lord that you will be kind to me and my family since I have helped you. Give me some guarantee that when Jericho is conquered, you will let me live, along with my father and mother, my brothers and sisters, and all their families." (Js 2:10-13)

Here we have the surrender of Rahab. Rahab, like Jericho and the whole land of Canaan, are not outside of us; they are inside. In the process of deliverance, mapping disarms the enemy, removes all of his resistance. Once this happened, the walls of Jericho collapsed. This is the power of spiritual mapping when dealing with the dark areas of the soul: it confirms the state of terror and defeat of the enemy.

We all know how the story of Rahab ended. Her intercession saved the lives of her entire family. They were all under the protection of the scarlet rope. One's personal deliverance always produces a collective impact. Amazingly, Rahab's deliverance placed her in the messianic genealogy and she became the great-grandmother of King David.

All because she welcomed the spies in peace. She responded transparently and accountably to the spiritual mapping process. She sincerely hosted those sent by God. She allowed them access to all areas of her life. She even risked her life, hiding them in her house: *"she had taken them up to the roof and hidden them beneath bundles of flax she had laid out." (Js 2:6).*

Nothing was hidden, not even the dregs of the soul. Flax speaks of justice; in this case it speaks of human justice, the sophistry that corrupted Rahab and caused her to become a prostitute. Her corrupted heart, the disarray of her soul, the intimate motives that supported her style of life that allowed her to live with her conscience... they were all exposed. Everything was brought out into the light – these were the conditions offered by the spies. Spiritual mapping became the decisive factor in the conquest of Canaan and in the transformation of Rahab. It changed the history of Israel and Rahab; it set the descendants of both on a different path.

I. INHERITANCE

Analyze the abuses, injustices, sinful connections, traumas that follow the same pattern of activity, wounds, etc. As demonstrated by the diagram, the field of inheritance is quite extensive, ranging from the genealogical history up to four generations (not more than that), until the age of reason.

1. Sphere of mapping of generational iniquities (past pedigree that spans three to four generations).

For the sake of our didactic strategy, we will be repeating some concepts that we have touched on earlier.

Just as there is a genetic, material, financial and cultural inheritance, there is also a spiritual heritage that is expressed in the form of either demonic (persecution) or divine (promises) visitation. When God appeared to Moses, he did it by using the following words to define his relationship with us: "I am the Lord God, the God of Abraham, Isaac and Jacob." There are two implications that come from this:

• *A personal relationship.*

God relates with us personally, as He related personally with Abraham, Isaac and Jacob. We are not a number in the crowd. God knows us by name, speaks to us individually. In fact, of all the religions of the world, the only God who is infinite and personal at the same time is the God of the Bible.

• *A generational relationship.*

God relates to us from a perspective of generations. The reason God appeared to Moses was the same reason He had His relationship with his ancestors Abraham, Isaac and Jacob. Even the words He used with them were the words He used with Moses; even though four hundred years had passed, God was there to keep the promises He made to Abraham and that He had confirmed with Isaac and Jacob. This promise extended to all of their descendants. The following text formulates the law of spiritual heritages.

PERSONAL MAPPING

I- FIEL OF INHERITANCE

Sphere of mapping of generational iniquities

History of conception

Birt history

History of gestation

6 to 9 months

History of childhood until the age of reason

Age of reason

II- FIELD OF RESPONSABILITY

Conscious choices

History of life after the age of reason

Current age

| Avós | Pais | Início da vida | Parto | 6 a 7 anos |

III- FIELD OF TERRITORIALITY (CRIMES OF BLOOD)

*History of the place (Conutry, city, state, property): - Crimes, murders, suicides, abortions, adulteries, practice of sexual perversion, occult rituals involving the invocation of demons, idolatry the consecration of "saints," sacrifices and offerings to spirits, and similar things can bring serious spiritual disorders that will damn a place. All of these things legalize a satanic territorial demarcation.

*Government sins and iniquities | *Church sins and iniquities

"... I, the Lord your God, am a jealous God who will not tolerate your affection for any other gods. I lay the sins of the parents upon their children; the entire family is affected—even children in the third and fourth generations of those who reject me. But I lavish unfailing love for a thousand generations on those who love me and obey my commands." (Ex 20:5-6)

The essence of iniquity is idolatry, i.e., someone who bows and serves something or someone that is occupying the place that belongs only to God. When iniquity is not redeemed, it will produce a latent influence, causing the children to make the same mistakes committed by parents.

This text establishes two types of spiritual heritage that we can receive and leave in relation to our family line:

— *"... I lavish unfailing love for a thousand generations on those who love me and obey my commands."*

It speaks of an abundance of promises that can be accumulated as an inheritance for our posterity. This is one of the most important statements of the Bible. We need to be aware of the impact that our obedience can cause on thousands of future generations. It is an incalculable benefit. What responsibility! Based on this passage, I always say that at some point we will stop talking about hereditary curses and begin to speak only about hereditary blessings!

— *"... I lay the sins of the parents upon their children; the entire family is affected — even children in the third and fourth generations of those who reject me."*

When the Bible says that God visits the sin of the fathers on the children up to the third and fourth generation, it is intelligently tracing the limit within which spiritual mapping needs to be drawn up. This is very practical. Imagine if we had to map the spiritual history of our ancestors back to Adam; we would be facing a task humanly impossible. However, as a family curse is highly symptomatic, it is sufficient to look at our relatives back just three or four generations and a spiritual diagnosis of our family will be is evident.

For example, if you spiritually look at the history of: 1. Grandparents; 2. Parents and uncles; 3. Brothers and cousins; and 4. Children and nephews, you will have a field which spans four generations. When moral law states that the iniquity of the fathers tends to repeat in the behavior of children through the third and fourth generation, it assumes an ability to map that offers full power of observation. For a spiritual diagnosis, this is smart, sensible and very practical.

This is a fundamental principle of deliverance that helps us identify the most remote generational sins that have flowered over a 3 or 4-generation span. As a result, personal and collective repentance, intelligent confessions and an effective intercession transform the situation, changing the heavens over the family and its descendants.

An understanding of hereditary mapping (genogram) is fundamental to being able to insert ourselves into the breach for our family through prophetic intercession and intercessory repentance. The

Field of Hereditary Mapeament

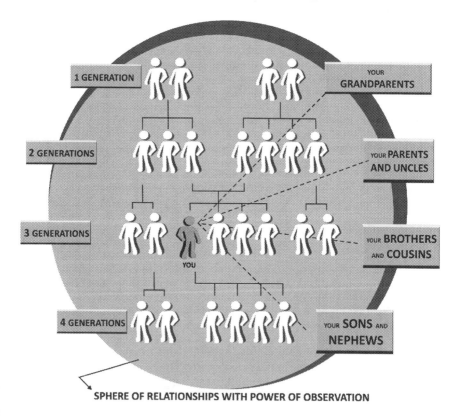

1 GENERATION	YOUR GRANDPARENTS
2 GENERATIONS	YOUR PARENTS AND UNCLES
3 GENERATIONS	YOU	YOUR BROTHERS AND COUSINS
4 GENERATIONS	YOUR SONS AND NEPHEWS

SPHERE OF RELATIONSHIPS WITH POWER OF OBSERVATION

Bible is full of these genograms and genealogies that reveal human and spiritual roots and behavioral addictions. Having access to this historical information about people, cities and nations, the intercessor can wisely fulfill his priestly role of restoring the ancient places that have been devastated through the generations.

This chronological field of 3 to 4 generations does not appear in the Bible by chance; it is not just unintentional data. No biblical information is merely casual. God knows what he says. While there is a chronological nature to it, more importantly, it dissects the makeup of the family's relationships so it can be examined in a more useful and efficient manner. Pay particular attention to this. This is a manner that God uses to alert us to the injustice that has accumulated in the spiritual inventory of the preceding generations. Our text explains that this is defined as God's zeal: *"... I, the Lord your God, am a jealous God who will not tolerate your affection for any other gods. I lay the sins of the parents upon their children..."*

We need to be attentive to the spiritual information the genogram furnishes – the access, intimacy, knowledge and power of observation. It is not difficult to construct a four-generational genogram of your family, identifying each person, spiritually relevant facts about them and the nature and significance of family relationships. For example, it is natural that we know our grandparents, parents and uncles/aunts, siblings and cousins and our children and nephews. That alone gives us four generations that may be simultaneously alive and present in our reality. Our family sphere of relationships typically spans four distinct generations.

Reiterating, we do not need more than 3 or 4 generations to take a reading of our spiritual heritage. Everything that happened previous to that, and that has not been spiritually redeemed, will be present in the last 3 or 4 generations. Symptoms flourish. It makes no sense that we would have to go rummaging through ancient generations to discover a hidden iniquity that would be the key to our deliverance. God zealously set up the essence of moral and civic law in the Ten Commandments and limited the mapping process to a maximum of four generations. This allows us to diagnose the latent symptoms of curses and their respective causes. It shows us the spiritual "disorders" that the more distant generations did not redeem and that now need to be addressed.

The Bible wisely provides us with a handy focus for the mapping of generational iniquities and their respective attacks they have opened up. These iniquities and corresponding attacks form our hereditary spiritual baggage that needs to be crucified; the mapping process allows us to see what needs to be done. From this type of research we can easily extract relevant, strange and unusual facts that clarify or confirm obvious symptoms of the propagation of hereditary iniquities, spiritual attacks and even demonic infestations.

Obviously, the essential aspect of mapping our generational history is to understand how this system of relationships and behaviors functions so we can assume our responsibility, affect the changes that we need to make in a healthy way and influence our family and relatives. This is where we need to invest more effort. It is important to understand that we develop our personality by being immersed in a system comprised of patterns that have been repeating for several generations. Mapping gives us the clarity to evaluate the problematic behavior and enables us to position ourselves so as to stop the activity and begin the re-education process so the behavior does not return.

Note that the principle source of spiritual mapping is God himself. Often, God is revealing things about our family to us; unfortunately, it is not unusual that we do not understand or we do not know what to do with the revelations when we receive them.

Hereditary mapping is one of the principle keys to the deliverance of a family. It is the aim of intercessory confession and provides dependable family counseling. In this manner, vital revelations that have been hidden and defended by demons housed in the family lineage are brought into the light.

"And I will give you treasures hidden in the darkness— secret riches. I will do this so you may know that I am the Lord, the God of Israel, the one who calls you by name." (Is 45:3)

Through research and the revelation of God, behavioral addictions are challenged and intercessory confessions break curses. Causes that have been ignored for decades, and longer, are uncovered and eliminated.

The first thing that needs to be understood is that the biblical response to dealing with hereditary curses comes through an intelligent confession of their respective generational sin. Unfortunately, this has become a practice that has been totally lost over the centuries and limits the priestly role of the church in restoring the ancient places (situations) that have been suffered from generation to generation.

Iniquities not redeemed function as anchors that hold or limit the behavior of successive generations.

Ignorance in relation to the confession of generation sin feeds a demonic influence that can leave the future offspring in a hostage situation in relation to sinful behaviors. It creates a kind of collective memory that establishes certain sinful practices as family culture and can thereby cause entire societies to lose all contact with God.

It is noteworthy that all the men whom God himself appointed as intercessors have practiced intercessory confession for the iniquities that have accumulated over the generations. This is biblical a principle that few priests managed to rediscover. Look at this prayer of Daniel:

> *"In view of all your faithful mercies, Lord, please turn your furious anger away from your city Jerusalem, your holy mountain. All the neighboring nations mock Jerusalem and your people because of our sins and the sins of our ancestors. O our God, hear your servant's prayer! Listen as I plead. For your own sake, Lord, smile again on your desolate sanctuary." (Dn 9:16-17)*

The confessional realm of generational sins

So how many generations of sin can we Intercessorially confess? We need to use common sense to analyze this. The Bible not only establishes a realm for mapping curses back to three to four generations, but it also establishes the same in terms of ten to fourteen generations. These following texts and many others give us an indication of this:

*"If a person is illegitimate by birth, neither he nor his descendants for **ten generations** may be admitted to the assembly of the Lord. No Ammonite or Moabite or any of their descendants for ten generations may be admitted to the assembly of the Lord." (Dt 23:2-3)*

*"All those listed above include **fourteen generations** from Abraham to David, **fourteen** from David to the Babylonian exile, and **fourteen** from the Babylonian exile to the Messiah." (Mt 1:17)*

Again, it is important to emphasize that the Bible offers no blind or casual information. We need for God to give us the heart of an intercessor so we can understand these texts with sociological and spiritual intelligence. As we examine the records of Matthew, we can see that God took fourteen generations, from Abraham to David, to build a nation that would be His redemptive agent on the face of the Earth. During the reign of David, the nation of Israel reached its apogee, occupying the whole of the territory that God had promised to Abraham, and experienced the height of its glory and the fulfillment of the promises made to them as people.

According to the history, after the death of David, there began a process of spiritual decay that after fourteen generations resulted in the destruction of the nation. Under the government of Solomon's son Rehoboam, the kingdom was divided into two parts: Judah (two tribes) and Israel (ten tribes). Gradually, a subtle process of sin and idolatry crept in, culminating in the exile of the two nations. First Israel went into captivity in Assyria and later Judah was carried off into captivity in Babylon.

"I looked for someone who might rebuild the wall of righteousness that guards the land. I searched for someone to stand in the gap in the wall so I wouldn't have to destroy the land, but I found no one. (Ez 22:30)

As God himself explains in Ezekiel, for lack of intercessors, the nation of Israel, who had been carried away to Assyria, never returned and became known as "the ten lost tribes of the House of Israel." While in captivity in Babylon, some intercessors experimented with expressive ministries and this ensured that the nation would be pre-served and eventually returned to the promised land.

The Bible mentions how these intercessors humbled them-selves before God during the exile, confessing their sins and the sins of their fathers. They interceded for the process of decay that had been started fourteen generations previous to them. Men like Daniel, Nehemiah, Ezra, and many others acknowledged and sacerdotally confessed the generational inequalities perpetrated by these four-teen generations as Matthew explains: "fourteen [generations] from David to the Babylonian exile."

The story continues after the deportation to Babylon and another fourteen generations passed until the Redeemer arrived: "fourteen [generations] from the Babylonian exile to the Messiah."

Therefore, what has been mapped up to four generations can and must be confessed up to ten or fourteen generations. Obviously, this intercession will not exempt those generations of their guilt before God; but it does remove the right to attack successive generations. It establishes a breakpoint, a new heaven over future generations, a new spiritual reality free from the harmful influences of Satan.

Yom Kippur – Corporate fasting and generational confession

*"On October 31 the people assembled again, and this time they fasted and dressed in burlap and sprinkled dust on their heads. Those of Israelite descent separated themselves from all foreigners as **they confessed their own sins and the sins of their ancestors**. They remained standing in place for three hours while the Book of the Law of the LORD their God was read aloud to them. Then for three more hours they confessed their sins and worshiped the LORD their God." (Ne 9:1-3)*

Yom Kippur gives us a better understanding of this practice. The corporate confession of generational iniquities was established as a perpetual statute in Jewish culture (Lv 23:26-32). This still occurs to-day during the ceremony of Yom Kippur or "Day of Atonement." The House of Jacob, the family of Israel, meets annually on the Feast of Tabernacles and fasts in deep contrition, establishing a memorable concert with God.

The *Vidui*, or confession, is a part of paramount importance in Yom Kippur liturgy. During the Vidui all sins are confessed, with the participants representing all Jews and their past generations. The strength of the purification that occurs on that day has become known as the day when Satan is brought down from the heavens, ensuring God's blessings for the year (on the Jewish calendar) and to the successive generations.

To clarify, we should not confuse the confession of the iniquities of our ancestors with the consulting of dead ancestors. The first situation is biblical. The second situation, the consultation of ancestors is anti-biblical and must be rejected. This is the basis of the spiritism and occultism that permeates almost all major world religions such as Buddhism, Kardecism, Hinduism, etc., and enslaves millions of people.

In fact, the consultation of dead ancestors is a satanic version of the biblical principle of confessing, intercessorially, the unconfessed and unacknowledged iniquities of our ancestors. Many well-intentioned, but misinformed, people confuse these concepts through this distortion. Through this distortion the Church has been robbed of her priestly capacity. This important principle of intercession needs to be rediscovered and rescued by the church.

2. History of conception

Another important aspect of our spiritual heritage resides in human conception. The history of conception is the core of any individual's spiritual genesis. Several factors may be important in this sense, but they all revolve around the marriage alliance axis.

The basic principle for human conception is related to sex. Sex is something highly spiritual. A blood covenant that plays a key role in the lives of people legitimately married is implicit in a sexual relationship. Children and family are things so sacred that we can only generate them through a blood pact, an alliance that should continue a lifetime.

In relation to the conception of a child, we need to consider several situations that can negatively affect his spiritual environment. Basically, the problems here revolve around immorality, abuse, violence and corruption. Was the child planned or not; was he the fruit of a relationship bolstered by covenant marriage or was he was conceived in immorality: fornication, adultery, incest (abuse), rape (violence), prostitution (corruption) etc.? A child being conceived in any of these sinful situations has a demonic entryway established that will impact that child's life.

3. History of gestation

This is another fundamental component of our heritage; it is the formation process of all aspects of human life. The intrauterine mother-child connection establishes the basic parameters for all of the child's relationships. The more delicate the traumas that occur during this phase, the more serious are the consequences that are produced. Many forms of injustice and violence can negatively weigh on the organic, psycho-emotional and spiritual formation of the child. It is at this same stage, when God is forming and establishing his plan for the child, that Satan brings maximum effort to sabotage the process by placing the very people against the child who should be protecting and preserving him.

Some examples of this would be if the child was rejected or abandoned by parents due to an unwanted conception; if the parents verbalize the intention or made some attempt to exterminate the child by abortion; if the father or mother verbally rejected the sex of the child, expressing their frustration in this regard; if there was violence, physical abuse or beatings of the mother by the husband where the child (in the womb) suffered some physical aggression; if there was any kind of ritual or consecration of the child to idols during pregnancy, etc.

4. Birth history

By itself, the birth process is traumatic. Not only does it involve a change of environment but it is also a bloody passage that can be extremely painful. From a spiritual perspective, childbirth can be interpreted as a blood pact being made between mother and child.

At the time of delivery, several traumas, accidents and incidents can happen. It is not unusual for the mother, or someone involved in the childbirth such as a nurse or midwife, to invoke the help of spiritual entities. They make dedications and promises in exchange for things going well and inadvertently compromise the life, identity and fate of the newborn child to spirit beings that they may or may not have intended.

5. History of childhood until the age of reason

This phase comprises the initial process of maturation and learning. The blood covenant established at birth between mother and child is strengthened in breastfeeding. A deep affection and sense of protection and responsibility naturally emerge, capturing the heart of the parents. This develops the mysterious chemistry that is present in the love that creates a family.

This period, childhood until the age of reason, is another stage that also places us in an environment where our ability to choose and defend ourselves does not exist. As in pregnancy, the child continues totally dependent and vulnerable by virtue of parental responsibility or irresponsibility.

Emotional abuse, physical abuse, sexual abuse, abandonment, dedication of children to idols and many other extreme situations are dangers during this period. The law of inheritance ensures that each frivolous word uttered by a parent legalizes a demonic influence of the same nature in the life of the child.

II. RESPONSABILITY

Man is a spiritual being, self-conscious, free to make decisions, i.e., he is inherently endowed with responsibility. God created no human being as a victim unable to respond or to assume the consequences of their choices. Our thoughts determine our deeds, our deeds determine our habits, our habits determine our character and our character determines our destiny.

Biblically speaking, responsibility is morally predetermined, i.e., it is proportional to the level of light. In the kingdom of God, light equals responsibility. The concept of light includes a series of parameters such as insight, knowledge, experience, and maturity.

The greater the light, the greater the responsibility.

Another important aspect to understand is that ignorance does not exempt us from the consequences of breaking the law. This is a tough way to grow in light and responsibility. When a child who has never studied about the law of gravity falls down, his ignorance will not exempt him from possible injury. Despite not having been aware of the danger of gravity, he will suffer the consequences if he runs afoul of the law. He is not exempt.

The assumption of responsibility in the life of any person comes into force after the age of reason or accountability, which can vary in the range of 5 to 7 years old. In the course of life, many choices and sinful behaviors can produce moral weaknesses, emotional traumas and sinful ties. This is better understood when you consider the causes of curses as we did earlier.

III. TERRITORIALITY

When the apostle Paul exhorts the church of Ephesus on the subject of unrelenting anger, which is the root for murder, he points out that we should not give a *"foothold to the devil" (Ep 4:27)*. The word "foothold" (*topos*) literally means "jurisdiction," alluding to an area of the human soul that is uncontrolled, but can also mean a territory.

Basically, the Bible specifies four sins that harm the earth: immorality, idolatry, innocent bloodshed and apostasy. These sins bring four judgments: drought, famine, plague and the sword.

Blood crimes and injustices have the power to spiritually contaminate the land, giving the devil jurisdiction, i.e., a place. On several occasions the Bible shows events that confirm this. The first example is in the fall of the human race. The sin of Adam also directly affected the earth: *"...to the man he said, 'Since you listened to your wife and ate from the tree whose fruit I commanded you not to eat, the ground is cursed because of you.'" (Gn 3:17)*. Because of the murder of Abel, God said to Cain: *"No longer will the ground yield good crops for you, no matter how hard you work! From now on you will be a homeless wanderer on the earth." (Gn 4:12)*. Similarly, a terrible famine struck the city of Jerusalem for three long years and God himself reveals the reason to David: *"The famine has come because Saul and his family are guilty of murdering the Gibeonites." (2 Sm 21:1)*.

Crimes, murders, suicides, abortions, adulteries, practice of sexual perversion, occult rituals involving the invocation of demons, idolatry, the consecration of "saints," sacrifices and offerings to spirits, and similar things can bring serious spiritual disorders that will damn a place. All of these things legalize a satanic territorial demarcation.

Demonic spirits are manipulating the mindset of our society in order to, with the goal of creating chaos with and in people's behavior, disturb them and even drive them mad.

Demonic influence is limited territorially by the person responsible for committing the crime or transgression and it is those acts or behaviors that enable the demonic influence to exert authority over the jurisdiction or property (Dt 21:1-9). The action of demons is restricted to the territory. The same principles and mechanisms used to free a person can and should be used to free a territory or property.

PRINCIPLES AND DEMONIC MANIFESTATIONS IN DELIVERANCE

People often give exaggerated importance to demonic manifestations or demonstrations. We must not, however, assess the success of a deliverance by the events that occur or fail to occur. The key point that triggers deliverance is based on the principles that are exercised with sincerity and consistency. Principles are reliable; manifestations are not. Never assume that a demonic manifestation is more important than an attitude of walking by faith and obedience.

A key aspect in the mapping process is knowing how to receive guidance and the ability to correctly read the symptoms and events presented during a session. Demonic manifestations should inspire us to investigate, confirm, monitor and confront.

Investigate

The main role of symptoms that can occur during a deliverance counseling session is to point us to where we need to dig deeper. Manifestations such as pain, stinging pricks, severe dizziness, gagging, vomiting, cold, heat and even critical situations of demonization during a deliverance session can orient us to a direction to be followed or can confirm that something has been or is being released or expelled.

It is common that during a deliverance session we have a vast field that needs to be investigated, but there are specific "hooks" on which demonic exploitation is based. If we do not uncover and dispose of these hooks, the ability to attain full freedom will be compromised.

Confirm

Some manifestations that occur during deliverance serve to confirm that the demonic stronghold that exists has been penetrated and broken. It can be obvious that something substantial has happened for the person and his family.

Monitor

A manifestation can also be invaluable in helping the person to maintain their newfound freedom. Because of it, they are now on alert to these areas of greater vulnerability and can redouble the efforts at vigilance.

This is a very delicate area and one must use much discernment. Just as God can utilize a demonic demonstration, so the devil can also take advantage of these events. He will attempt to bring confusion and divert, even subtly, the person who is guiding the freedom session to take a different path, detouring him away from the real issue. This effectively serves to prolong the process, wear out the liberator, wear down the counselee and frustrate the desired results.

Another thing to be aware of is that along with these strong symptoms that occur you can see an orchestrated attack of pride and self-sufficiency levied against the liberator, especially if a person is still immature. This moves them away from dependence on God and reliance on themselves. This is always disastrous.

Confront

Perhaps surprisingly, a demonic manifestation that occurs in a deliverance session can also have a prophetic character in relation to others who are present. That is, God allows the demonstration so that someone present besides the counselee may be edified, comforted or even confronted. I have experienced this on multiple occasions and have even seen some participants receiving a deliverance as profound and intense as the counselee's.

3

CAUSES OF CURSES

Many of us think that while God established the principle of blessing, curses were established by the devil. But this is not what the Bible says. As mentioned earlier, the principles of both were established by God and are respectively triggered by human choices. The devil is nowhere close to being the star in this show.

> *"Today I have given you the choice between life and death, between blessings and curses. Now I call on heaven and earth to witness the choice you make. Oh, that you would choose life, so that you and your descendants might live!" (Dt 30:19)*

It is very important to demystify something in the field of spiritual warfare. If you carefully study the Bible you will realize that the devil never appears as the main character in human affairs. In fact, there are very few biblical passages that refer to him at all. Being biblically studious, we will eventually arrive at the terrifying conclusion that we are our own worst enemies! Therefore, the cause of curses is actually human. Additionally, it is not the devil who attacks the earth with curses, but it is God himself, dealing with human rebellion!

Our responsibility is not above our affiliation. Adam as the Son of God was formed by His hands, but because he disobeyed, God drove him out of the garden and deprived him of living forever. It is logical that God forgave him, but the consequent curse of death remained on Adam and all his offspring. We cannot assume that God will not do the same with us.

The spiritual realm, while not immediate, is accurate. Sin is never isolated from the curse. The wages of sin is death. The serpent attempted to tell the woman otherwise, but the result was still death. Therefore, this part of our diagram needs to be taken seriously. In a very practical way we will enumerate some of the primary reasons that are usually present in demonic attacks or exploitation.

CAUSE 1. Iniquity of the parents – family inheritance

We carry the blessings and the curses of our ancestors. This may seem strange, but it is true. We ignore the law of inheritance found in the Bible because we read it, the Bible, from our westernized world-view. As westerners, we adopt an individualistic vision of life. The law of inheritance does not carry any relevant meaning to us. It seems odd to us that the sin of someone else can produce consequences for successive generations. It simply does not fit within our cultural context. However, culture is not above the Scripture.

While we can quibble about the many existing genealogies in the Bible, we can see the degree of importance that Israel gave to family heritage and its roots. The roots of a person also show the roots of their problems. Roots by nature are buried and are always well hidden.

This ignorance in relation to our family heritage is symptomatic. Iniquities of our parents that are not redeemed authorize a malignant influence of a corresponding nature over our lives and relationships. Ignoring this fact, we unnecessarily have to coexist with a series of misfortunes.

Belonging vs. Deserving
The principal conflict is that there is embedded in the law of inheritance a strange concept of justice that is not based on worthiness, but affiliation. For example, a woman who gives birth to a child with AIDS, why does her recklessness contaminate him? Did the child deserve to be born with AIDS? Was he at fault; obviously not. Is this fair? If not, is God unjust? The child does not shoulder the blame for AIDS but he does carry the consequence. This is not fatalism, but it is a fatality that is real. This is the power of the law of inheritance.

From a difference perspective, suppose a person has parents who were very successful in life and accumulated great wealth. The parents die and their entire fortune goes to the child. Is this fair?

What did this child do to deserve this? Did he even break a sweat to earn the fortune left him by his parents; of course not. Inheritance is a matter of affiliation, not merit.

The concept of justice based on worthiness is important, and even fundamental, in many situations of life, but it is not everything. This is one of the primary lessons taught in the parable of the prodigal son. Even without deserving it, he had a right to his inheritance. Inheritance is not linked to merit, it comes through affiliation. Similarly, the foundation of the right to salvation is not tied to merit but to affiliation. Jesus gave up the right to be the *"only begotten of the Father"* and, through his death and resurrection, became the *"firstborn among many brothers and sisters,"* including us in the family of God, making us heirs of God and co-heirs with Christ.

Truthfully, grace and mercy go against the grain of worthiness: grace is receiving the good that we do not deserve and mercy is not receiving the bad that we do deserve. This is the justice of the cross. If we sow this justice, by this justice we will reap the corresponding fruits: "God blesses those who are merciful, for they will be shown mercy."

Responsibility and inheritance are inseparable. Blessing and curses constitute the essence of the principle of spiritual heritage. Let's look at some biblical examples that confirm this immutable principle of God's Kingdom.

In the parable of the uncompassionate creditor, Jesus himself endorses this spiritual truth: *"He couldn't pay, so his master ordered that he be sold—along with his wife, his children, and everything he owned—to pay the debt." (Mt 18:25).*

Similarly, when Gehazi was corrupted and coveted Naaman's offer of riches, Elisha declared that the curse Gehazi was seeking to remove would now become his because of his attitude: *"Because you have done this, you and your descendants will suffer from Naaman's leprosy forever." When Gehazi left the room, he was covered with leprosy; his skin was white as snow." (2 Kg 5:27)*

Why would not just Gehazi become a leper? The Bible makes it clear that he would see the consequences of his sins in his lineage. What a responsibility!

The same thing happened to Achan when he coveted some spoils of battle that had been cursed and prohibited by God prior to the battle. His actions consequently brought defeat on Israel and death for himself and his entire household (Js 7:1-26). The consequences of his sin affected many innocent people.

The following text further clarifies the Jewish mindset about a hereditary curse: *"Pilate saw that he wasn't getting anywhere and that a riot was developing. So he sent for a bowl of water and washed his hands before the crowd, saying, "I am innocent of this man's blood. The responsibility is yours!" And all the people yelled back, "We will take responsibility for his death—we and our children!" (Mt 27:24-25).*

Both Pilate, as someone knowledgeable of the Jewish precepts, and the audience had a clear understanding that a curse automatically extends to one's offspring. After this declaration, the curse it invoked, has weighed heavily on each proceeding Jewish generation. From the massacre of Jerusalem in 70 A.D., where thousands were crucified and burned alive, to the holocaust of World War II, Jews have been persecuted, exiled, murdered, despised, hated, etc. Jesus demonstrated the same understanding when he pronounced a judgment on that generation: *"...As a result, you will be held responsible for the murder of all godly people of all time — from the murder of righteous Abel to the murder of Zechariah son of Barachiah, whom you killed in the Temple between the sanctuary and the altar" (Mt 23:35).*

As much as we may dislike the idea that our sins bring about a curse on our offspring, it does not change the immutable reality that exists in the spiritual world.

"You will die among the foreign nations and be devoured in the land of your enemies. Those of you who survive will waste away in your enemies' lands because of their sins and the sins of their ancestors." (Lv 26:38-39)

And your children will be like shepherds, wandering in the wilderness for forty years. In this way, they will pay for your faithlessness, until the last of you lies dead in the wilderness. (Nm 14:33)

Kill this man's children! Let them die because of their father's sins! They must not rise and conquer the earth, filling the world with their cities." (Is 14:21)

We need to understand what iniquity is. Iniquity carries two basic concepts: unredeemed or unconfessed sins repeat in every generation and the punishment associated with those sins will be applied to future generations.

Abraham provides a classic example of this. Have you ever wondered why the Israelites were slaves in Egypt for more than 300 years? How could the people of God, the seed blessed through Abraham, have been forced to become and remain slaves for so long?

When God called Abraham, he left the city of Ur of the Chaldeans and headed towards the land of Canaan (Gn 12:7). He arrived at Bethel where he built an altar to God (Gn 12:8). Afterwards Abraham faced an enormous test – a famine came on the land. It is not easy when God calls and sends you to a place of blessing and you are faced with hunger.

After leaving for the promised land, Abraham now leaves the promised land. The father of faith stumbled in disbelief and went down to Egypt. There he complicated everything. A lie resulted in the abduction of his wife. God released plagues on Pharaoh, who discovered the truth and gave Abraham a sermon. When the Pharaoh of Egypt has to preach to the Prophet of God, things have become ugly indeed! From there, Abraham returned to Canaan, orienting himself, as the Bible says, by old altars along the way.

The most interesting thing about Abraham's detour is that it would create the reality of his future descendants: *"Then the Lord said to Abram, "You can be sure that your descendants will be strangers in a foreign land, where they will be oppressed as slaves for 400 years." (Gn 15:13)*. Abraham's error cost his descendants 430 years of punishment in Egypt, 300 of which were spent in harsh slavery. This is exactly what the Bible is affirming!

Statistically, the tendency is to validate and transfer a sinful situation to the next generation, as we can see in the example of King Jeroboam's idolatry when Israel seceded from Judah. Jeroboam set in motion a legacy of idolatry that was installed in the reign of each of his successors and transmitted to the next king.

Each succeeding king repeated the sin of Jeroboam: Nadab (1 Kg 15:26), Baasha (1 Kg 16:1-2), Omri (1 Kg 16:25-26), Ahab (1 Kg 16:30-31), Ahaziah (1 Kg 22:52-54), Jehoahaz (2 Kg 13:1-2), Jehoash (2 Kg 13:10-11), Jeroboam II (2 Kg 14:23-24), Zacharias (2 Kg 15:8-

9), Pekahiah (2 Kg 15:23-24). Finally in the reign of Hoshea Israel is taken into captivity by Assyria (2 Kg 17:20-23) — the culmination of an uninterrupted curse that climaxed in the captivity and destruction of the nation. To this day the ten tribes who formed the nation of Israel remain scattered!

There was no intercessory discernment in any of these reigns that led them to confess the hereditary idolatry in order to stop the curse. This was the cry of God's heart: *"I looked for someone who might rebuild the wall of righteousness that guards the land. I searched for someone to stand in the gap in the wall so I wouldn't have to destroy the land, but I found no one" (Ez 22:30)*. The drastic conclusion that we can draw here is succinctly stated by God Himself: "My people are being destroyed because they don't know me" (Ho 4:6).

CAUSE 2. Breaking alliances

a) Breaking the wedding alliance – Adultery and divorce

"For I hate divorce!" [literally, repudiation] *says the Lord, the God of Israel. "To divorce your wife is to overwhelm her with cruelty," says the Lord of Heaven's Armies. "So guard your heart; do not be unfaithful to your wife" (Ml 2:16).*

Adultery and rejection are implicit in each other. These are the main mechanisms of the destruction of marriage and they leave a cursed consequence. Malachi expresses God's opinion about divorce through a pun: *"for I hate divorce,"* emphasizing that He detests detest, rejects rejection and is divorced from divorce. He further explains that adultery is the main aspect of divorce and it literally means *to be dressed in violence*. The burden of violence contained in a divorce is capable of destroying many preceding generations.

In the case of Abraham and Hagar, polygamy caused a family disruption that resulted in the expulsion of Hagar and her son. Combined with the development in the preceding generations of a growing conflict between the descendants of Ishmael and Isaac, who continue fighting to this day; world peace is threatened. This cultural war of terror between the Islamic bloc and the Judeo-Christian world began with a "simple" case of adultery that ended in rejection.

The implications of adultery

Lets internally analyze what happens when a marriage suffers a case of adultery. These are some of the possible curses that occur:

• Spiritual and ministerial marginalization of the person who committed adultery. Trying to figure out why men have a timid and inexpressive participation in churches in general, you will discover that a large proportion of them have lost the moral authority in their own family because of hidden adulteries. It is increasingly difficult in our churches (in Brazil) to find a man who can say: "I never betrayed my wife!"

• Adultery emotionally disrupts marriage, producing an obsession with jealousy, contempt, competition, chronic disagreements and all kinds of disruptions and distortions in the communication of the couple.

• Adultery is the breaking of an alliance, spiritually bringing a strange "person" into the marriage. It is not just the emotional presence of a lover; it is an actual demonic intrusion.

• Adultery also demonizes the marital bed, spiritually contaminating it. It produces for one or both of the spouses an inhibition, interruption or even sexual aversion by the other. It is the nature of the spirit of adultery to remove sexual pleasure from inside the marriage to the outside.

• Adultery removes sexual protection from the children of the couple, leaving them susceptible to various possibilities of harassment and sexual abuse. I have taken numerous informal polls and have confirmed this repeatedly. Many children are sexually abused in the same season in which one or both parents were engaged in adultery.

• The adultery of either spouse exposes the other, the victim of the treason, to the same situation. It is common, for example, in cases where the wife has committed adultery, to discover that her husband had, or has, secretly been doing the same for a long time.

• Adultery directly affects the family's financial life. Money begins to be diverted to immorality. The tendency is that the spirit of adultery takes the family to bankruptcy.

• Adultery implies the active ingredients of scandal and deception. Invariably every adulterer will have to face a time of exposure and scandal. It will occur sooner or later and in a more or less painful manner, depending on the person's attitude. The more a person cheats and avoids transparency and accountability, the worse the consequences become. The time factor only internalizes and intensifies the problem.

All cases of adultery, sooner or later, if not treated, will produce a chronic situation of familial deception, pain, rejection, divorce and abandonment.

A BIBLICAL PERSPECTIVE ABOUT DIVORCE

It is vitally important for those who are involved in the day-to-day running of a church to know how to bring common sense and biblical understanding to the context of divorce. The law of divorce exerts a civilizing function, helping to accommodate people directly or indirectly involved in these situations of extreme conflict and trauma.

First, it is important to establish the difference between rejection (renunciation or disavowal) and divorce. Understanding these concepts improves our perspective on the subject.

– **Rejection** (repudiation) involves dishonor, hatred, separation, adultery, betrayal, abandonment of the home, threat, violence, the lack of wanting reconciliation, etc. All this comes from the hardness of the heart. This is what God hates, as the prophet Malachi states. It is when the heart intentionally abandons the relationship.

– **Divorce** is the simple document that is given after an appropriate process formalizes the decision of one or both of the spouses to renounce or disavow the marriage. What is really at stake is not divorce, it is rejection.

Rejection is a moral failure; divorce is a legal device. In many situations there is a conflict between the moral and legal. These are difficult issues. Divorce legalizes separation, but there is a spiritual aspect to this. In many cases the legal is absurdly immoral; though it may be socially acceptable, it is spiritually reprehensible.

Until death separates us

There is a famous saying that states: "Open your eyes before getting married because afterwards they will have to be closed to a lot." Once you are married there is no point in claiming that the marriage "wasn't of God;" if it was not, it came to be! You made your choice, now you have to live with it! God is not pleased with fools (Ec 5:1-2).

It is not easy to deal with divorce, to salvage what you can while attempting to minimize the traumatic aftereffects. However, we have to remember the basic consequence of divorce. The Bible explains that the husband is connected to his wife by the law of marriage until death separates them (1 Co 7:39).

Therefore, any spouse who hardens his heart, rejects the other, dishonors the marriage covenant, abandons the home permanently, opts for divorce, is invoking death itself, as it is written: *"until death do them part."* This is the curse of divorce. This will affect all areas of life, creating moral failure, disappointment and widespread scandal, loss of family members (children), financial losses, emotional disturbances, spiritual death, ministerial destruction, traumatized relationships, etc. There are no winners in divorce.

Marriage is the school of character, the primary test for real maturity, and it involves a blood alliance for life. Unfortunately, a high percentage of couples fail in this test and become one of the primary riddles that the government of the church must address.

The law of divorce

After centuries of slavery in Egypt, facing the tough task of restoring the foundations of the nation, easing so many wounds and social disorders, civilly rearranging the family, Moses legalized divorce. The ideal is that a law like this did not need to exist, but as there is no perfect society, it was eventually instituted.

For a long time this law fulfilled its civilizing role. Then Jesus himself in the New Testament brings a serious complaint against it. In fact, the entire religious system of Israel, symbolized by the fig tree which Jesus cursed and that dried up at the roots, was deeply corrupt (Matthew 23). The law of divorce, as well as other laws, was distorted in order to meet the interest of those who applied them.

Therefore, in the case of divorce, it is necessary to give a warning as Jesus did in confronting the Pharisees (Mt 19:8) that, despite it being biblically legal, divorce can become a dangerous device, distortive, abusive, easily used with corrupt motives, inspired by selfishness, indiscreet, lustful, vain, irresponsible, malevolent and used as a device for revenge.

For this reason it is important to consider the context of the statements made by Jesus about divorce in the Gospels. They were made to confront religious leaders who unscrupulously were making divorce a pretext for rejection and thus perverting the functionality of the law. The law of divorce was instituted because of rejection, not to be a pretext for it. Anyone who is looking in the Bible for a justification for divorcing is traveling the wrong road! It is the road to a hard heart!

Pay attention to this: God did not institute separation. This came about through the initiative of man, the hardness of his heart, as Jesus stated. Despite the fact that God has forbidden separation (*what God has joined together, let no one separate*), the law of divorce regulated it. God never said that there could be separations and neither did He give His permission for it. This was never His purpose. He only said that since a separation already exists that it should be formalized; there must be a settlement, a formal satisfaction made for society. The law of Divorce has no **authoritative** character, only a **normative** one.

One spouse should not simply abandon the other, just as they should not simply cohabit without a marriage covenant that involves both families. If there is to be a separation, it should follow an appropriate standard. It is a matter of civility. It needs to be understood that a divorce does not exempt someone from the consequent curses associated with it; it only formalizes the new situation in the eyes of society. What we can do in counseling after a divorce is to try to minimize those consequences.

After separation (rejection), divorce was forbidden only if the husband unjustly accused his wife of infidelity or if the man was compelled to marry because he had disgraced the girl (Dt 22:13-29). Without a divorce, they would be legally prevented from contracting a new marriage.

In Leviticus 21:7, we see a restriction on the marriage of divorced priests and in Ezekiel 44:21-22 the same restriction is also extended to widows: *"The priests must not drink wine before entering the inner courtyard. They may choose their wives only from among the virgins of Israel or the widows of the priests. They may not marry other widows or divorced women."*

This is a very wise precept. I have seen this up close many times. Anyone who has a ministerial call, i.e., is in active ministry and holds a leadership role in the church should not marry a divorcee or widow who was not previously married to someone who was also in ministry. A second marriage usually has conflicts between ex-family and the new spouse or is impacted by the lack of acceptance by children and stepchildren. This can create all sorts of "situations," damage and embarrassment for the ministry and the church. At the very least, the new partner has an understanding of the constraints of ministry and will not be caught off guard by these disruptions and problems when they occur.

In relation to people in general, the Mosaic divorce law had only one impediment for a new marriage and it was directed towards a couple that had already been married to each other. The law provided for successive marriages and divorces, as is unfortunately happening today:

> "Suppose a man marries a woman but she does not please him. Having discovered **something wrong** with her, he writes her a letter of divorce, hands it to her, and sends her away from his house. When she leaves his house, she is free to marry another man. But if the second husband also turns against her and divorces her, or if he dies, the first husband may not marry her again, for she has been defiled. That would be detestable to the Lord. You must not bring guilt upon the land the Lord your God is giving you as a special possession" (Dt 24:1-4).

The body of this law allows us to draw some conclusions:

1. The legitimate reason for divorce is mentioned in general terms, alluding to something morally reprehensible or immoral: "...Having discovered **something wrong** (erwãh dabhar)."

The Hebrew terminology erwãh dabhar occurs as a phrase only in Deuteronomy 23:14: "The camp must be holy, for the Lord your God moves around in your camp to protect you and to defeat your enemies. He must not see any **shameful thing** among you, or he will turn away from you." The same type of indecent situation that causes God to separate Himself from us is what supposedly "justifies" a husband to separate from his wife. This is the original meaning of terminology.

Jesus seems to endorse this same attitude: *"... unless she has been unfaithful" (Mt 5:32)*. However, as the Bible does not conclusively establish a motive for divorce — and I believe that this is deliberate — and because each case is a case, my opinion is that one should try in every way possible to restore the marriage, even in the case of adultery. Many marriages have been saved even after the mortal wound of adultery. We will explore the intricacies of how to handle this in the next chapter.

I personally think that the only caveat for separation and divorce is if one spouse is in serious danger of being harmed or killed. If there is a history of threats and assaults that demonstrate this, we are dealing with a case for the police. Under those circumstances the person has no choice but to separate. Sadly, this situation occurs more frequently than we imagine.

2. A new marriage is prohibited between the same people who were married to each other and divorced: *"...the first husband may **not marry her again**, for she has been defiled."*

For reasons that I do not understand, the Bible prohibits restoring a marriage that has been the victim of divorce. It argues that this spiritually contaminates the land. Stated differently, it demonizes the territory and indicates that this occurrence would only worsen society as a whole.

Bringing this current, it is worth pointing out that there are abusive situations that exist where a church obligates a divorced person (who was divorced before they knew Jesus) to return to the first spouse. It does not matter that there may be children involved or that the former spouse may now be remarried. This simply adds more confusion and is not a solution; the reality is that it is an insupportable option and will only drive the person from church. This type of doctrine is the exact opposite of the biblical intention and constitutes a spiritual illegality: *"may not marry her again."* This is more than legalism; it is "illegalism." This transforms a bad situation into a worse one.

When a person becomes a believer in Jesus and is subjugated to such unnecessary tyranny, the obvious outcome is rejection, self-condemnation, bitterness and apostasy. Instead of providing comfort, support and direction, the church becomes guilty of killing her own wounded.

Even God Himself is impacted by this restriction of not returning to a former spouse once divorced. Constrained by His infinite love He states:

> *"If a man divorces a woman and she goes and marries someone else, he will not take her back again, for that would surely corrupt the land. But you have prostituted yourself with many lovers, so why are you trying to come back to me?" says the Lord" (Je 3:1).*

3. Divorce implies the possibility of another marriage: *"sends her away from his house. When she leaves his house, she is **free to marry another man.**"*

We cannot ignore this issue. It is essential that wise counsel be brought into these situations. While the concept of second marriages is implicit in the law of divorce, God never intended this for the family relationship. These situations always leave serious collateral damage involving children, finances, stepchildren, spouses, etc. The consequences of a divorce are always landmines and the demands of a second marriage are usually complicated.

I personally hold a radical position against separation and divorce; I have never advised or counseled someone to separate and divorce. However, we do not have the option of burying our heads in the sand and ignoring what is happening. There are hundreds of thousands of people already in this situation and they are flooding our churches. What good is it to simply condemn them?

If we are going to have a hope of solving or mitigating the consequences of these situations, we must bring insight and common sense to the table when dealing with issues such as divorce, remarriage, cohabitating, etc. Pastorally it requires much effort, balance and wisdom from God. There is no absolute rule that can be applied as a "recipe" to all cases. Each case is a case. The experience of one situation does not necessarily apply to another.

The process of redeeming a history of divorce requires that we construct an equation with multiple variables and apply resolve: Who rejected whom? Who abandoned the home? Was there adultery involved? Are there children that resulted from the adultery? Were there threats of violence or actual violence? Did the divorce occur before or after the new birth? Does the person occupy a leadership position in the church? Are there children? Has the spouse already remarried? Does the possibility of reconciliation exist? ...

There is no way to build a solution that involves all of that. My goal is to simply outline the biblical basics and guidelines so that we can better understand the spirit of the law, enhance our ability to contextualize it and construct the best possible solutions in each case.

It is important to constructively raise some specific questions when counseling the divorced, especially those who have remarried: what can be done today to alleviate the wounds and enhance the relationships that are affected? How do you behave in front of children with whom you have lost contact because of the divorce? What can you do to fix the mistakes you made in the first marriage so that the situation is not repeated in an even worse manner in the second marriage? What needs to be changed in your character? ...

Two extremes

There are two highly destructive extremes that exist in relation to divorce and a second marriage:

1. People who remarry and unscrupulously act as though nothing happened in the first marriage.

To marry a second time as though nothing occurred in the first marriage is to invite and reinforce infidelity, immorality and the loss of family ties. It is highly destructive and causes the breakdown of both the family and society in general. Unfortunately, this has become the norm and occurs repeatedly, openly welcoming the return of adultery and creating the vicious cycle that leads to the familiar path of pain and destruction.

2. People who condemn the second marriage, expressly excluding it from the norm of the Scriptures.

It is worth repeating that in many cases second marriages should be condemned because the person is living in adultery; however, in others the divorce is actually a highly redemptive mechanism for the person who was injured, rejected, betrayed, assaulted, abandoned, and/or helpless in their marriage. The sad reality is that in some cases divorce is the only remaining alternative:

> *"She saw that I divorced faithless Israel because of her adultery. But that treacherous sister Judah had no fear, and now she, too, has left me and given herself to prostitution" (Je 3:8).*

It is God Himself speaking in this text. He did not divorce Israel on His own initiative; rather, it was Israel's stubborn rebellion and rejection of Him. She rejected the Lord, exchanging Him for her lovers. God does not ignore this type of pain. After being rejected, He instituted through a divorce and remarriage with the church:

> *And the Lord said, "Name him Lo-ammi—'Not my people'—for Israel is not my people, and I am not their God." Yet the time will come when Israel's people will be like the sands of the seashore—too many to count! Then, at the place where they were told, 'You are not my people,' it will be said, 'You are children of the living God' (Ho 1:9-10).*

This divine verdict illustrates God's divorce of His people and His marriage to a people who had no relationship with Him. The new alliance produced a new Israel. It is no longer based on a physical descendency from Abraham; it is now available to an innumerable spiritual offspring that can include anyone, of any nationality, who has an open heart to believe and obey as Abraham did: *"For you are not a true Jew just because you were born of Jewish parents or because you have gone through the ceremony of circumcision" (Rm 2:28).*

Whether we like it or not, whether we accept it or not, regardless of its consequences, divorce and remarriage were regulated in the Bible. To say otherwise is exaggerating the law, de-civilizing society, debunking grace and banning mercy. While this may seem to be very spiritual, it can be highly destructive.

Recently I had to address a situation of a young man who was very devoted to God. Just a few months after marrying, his wife fell in love with a person at their church and simply abandoned him. He tried unsuccessfully in every way imaginable to restore the marriage. Even worse his wife had become pregnant by this other person. Divorce and hardness of the heart were not the heart of this husband. His wife rejected him and his attempts to restore their relationship. In the light of this, prohibiting him from marrying again is wanting to be more just than God Himself. It is pure legalism. It is destructive! Once being rejected by his spouse, he is now rejected by the church, and in the name of God for good measure. Obviously each situation must be analyzed very carefully.

Government and service

To be unfaithful to our spouse is to be unfaithful to God. Anyone who wants to take God seriously needs to take marriage seriously. Ministry is associated with testimony and moral credibility. Authority and testimony are proportional values. Without testimony authority does not exist. The words become empty. It is the letter without the spirit, the truth without coherence, which ends up being discredited. The lack of authority removes impact from ministry and makes it irrelevant.

Many who come into our churches are already in their second or third marriages. Others are divorced after becoming believers, which is terrifying from a number of perspectives. All relative details pertinent to each situation must be considered when opportunities for service in the local church are created for these people.

The Bible does not hinder anyone from serving; it does place conditions on leadership. If a person's history demonstrates difficulties in relation to his role as the head of the family, he should be given a serving position and not one of leadership. He does not have the moral infrastructure or the biblical endorsement to fulfill the function of leadership and to provide spiritual covering for others. The apostle Paul noted that if someone cannot govern his own house, he has no business attempting to govern the church (1 Tm 3:5). The restriction is here on leadership, not service. What limits service is one's testimony.

b) Bastard children - propagating the curse

Conceiving children outside the protection of the marriage covenant generates rejection, segregation and a compulsive and precocious immorality.

"If a person is illegitimate by birth, neither he nor his descendants for ten generations may be admitted to the assembly of the Lord" (Dt 23:2).

Moses explains that illegitimately birthed children are not allowed to enter the congregation of the Lord. There is a spiritual disturbance that is generated. A spiritually demonic influence is installed and it produces a resistance. This resistance hinders the person of becoming part of the divine process of marriage, family and church (Assembly of the Lord). It releases a matrix of spiritual attack that is emotional, sexual and even homosexual. It attempts to make the person precociously reproduce the same situation by which he was conceived.

This sin-propagation mechanism can produce a social impact that is able to affect up to ten generations. In many cultures around the world, primarily in the third world, this situation that Moses denounced is commonplace. In some regions in Brazil, for example, it is common to see women who have become mothers by the time they are thirteen years old, grandmothers by twenty-six and great grandmothers by thirty-nine. This type of curse brings incalculable social damages and multiples misery and violence.

c) Breaking the covenant with God: Apostasy

There is a list of more than 50 verses in Deuteronomy 28 that contain curses coming as the result of apostasy. Apostasy is the worse type of covenant breaking because of its effects on one's eternal salvation. Both Hosea and the apostle Paul call it a type of spiritual prostitution that invokes God's hardest punishment and corrections.

Apostasy explains much about the moral decline of society. Invariably, people who fall away become much worse than they were before experimenting with the Truth. For four years I made evangelistic visits to a psychiatric hospital and one of the things that impressed me most was the high percentage of "former-evangelicals" who were interred. They were the most disturbed patients in the hospital. Apostasy brings a series of curses related to the psycho-emotional disintegration, depression and panic:

"The Lord will strike you with madness, blindness, and panic" (Dt. 28:28).

3 | CAUSES OF CURSES

PART II - ANALYSING THE DIAGRAM

INTELLIGENT SHEPHERDING

"There among those nations you will find no peace or place to rest. And the Lord will cause your heart to tremble, your eyesight to fail, and your soul to despair. Your life will constantly hang in the balance. You will live night and day in fear, unsure if you will survive. In the morning you will say, 'If only it were night!' And in the evening you will say, 'If only it were morning!' For you will be terrified by the awful horrors you see around you" (Dt. 28:65-67).

"And for those of you who survive, I will demoralize you in the land of your enemies. You will live in such fear that the sound of a leaf driven by the wind will send you fleeing. You will run as though fleeing from a sword, and you will fall even when no one pursues you" (Lv. 26:36).

CAUSE 3. Idolatry

All sin is a violation of some kind of relationship. Idolatry is a sin against God Himself. It is a faith based on a lie and vanity — a distorted faith — that insidiously and malignantly distorts what may have begun as real faith. There are two curses that are imposed by idolatry:

• The idolater becomes the idol

Idolatry involves an alteration of one's identity. For the person who pays homage to an idol, the idol becomes a walking, talking, listening entity while the person becomes spiritually blind, deaf, dumb, inert and as insensitive as the idol. The more the idol becomes real for the person, the more the person becomes as passive and subjugated as the idol. This is an inviolable law of the spiritual world: we are transformed into the likeness of what we believe.

"Their idols are merely things of silver and gold, shaped by human hands. They have mouths but cannot speak, and eyes but cannot see. They have ears but cannot hear, and noses but cannot smell. They have hands but cannot feel, and feet but cannot walk, and throats but cannot make a sound. And those who make idols are just like them, as are all who trust in them" (Ps 115:4-8).

It is quite common to see people who have had major involvement with idolatry or have carried images in religious processions to have issues with fractures, intense pain in their joints, pains and weight in their spine and extreme spiritual blindness. They become as rigid, brittle and insensitive as the images they love and trust.

• Deception and spiritual exposure

Whenever we go to God or we seek Him via the idols of our heart, we will be caught in a snare. We will be fooled and become victims of our own idolatry: *"Tell them, 'This is what the Sovereign Lord says: The people of Israel have set up idols in their hearts and fallen into sin, and then they go to a prophet asking for a message. So I, the Lord, will give them the kind of answer their great idolatry deserves" (Ez 14:4).* When it come to idolatry, God Himself encourages the deception of our heart — this is one of the worst types of judgment we can be under.

Using this loophole, demonic entities camouflage themselves in the character or personality of saints, dead relatives, orishas (spirits), etc. The grand trick of Satan is religion. It is not surprising that the greatest atrocities in history have been perpetrated in the name of religion.

Idolatry is the branch of occultism that works in the area of protection. People come to it seeking protection and favors from a spiritual source that is not the true God. Ironically, what actually happens is that in the very area the devotee is seeking protection or favor, these entities play an opposite role and cause a growing spiritual dependency on them. It is not unlike the relationship between a drug dealer and a junkie.

For this reason it is common to observe people devoted to St. Christopher (protector of motorists) suffer countless automobile accidents, people committed to St. Antonio (protector of marriage) divorced several times or unable to find a spouse, people devoted to St. Valentine (protector of love) falling into sentimental and familial disgrace, people devoted to the St. Luzia (protector of eyes) suffering from eye problems or sentimental blindness, people devoted to St. Jude Thaddeus, the saint of impossible causes, are always facing irreversible loss and disaster, and so on.

CAUSE 4. Rebellion and dishonoring parents

This is a highly relevant point. All behavior inspired by contempt and the dishonoring of parents is strongly cursed: *"Cursed is anyone who dishonors father or mother.' And all the people will reply, 'Amen'"* *(Dt 16:27)*. Situations such as involvement with drugs, lies, verbal and physical aggression against parents, marriage without the consent of parents and so on entail harsh consequences. Among them are:

• Chronic disgrace
"...If a man has a hundred sheep and one of them gets lost, what will he do? Won't he leave the ninety-nine others in the wilderness and go to search for the one that is lost until he finds it?" (Lk 15:14). This was the curse of the prodigal son. He despised his father, wildly and irresponsibly spent his inheritance and was reduced to a state of miserable poverty. His lot was the land of famine and scarcity.

• Blindness and suffering
"If you insult your father or mother, your light will be snuffed out in total darkness" (Pr 20:20). A lack of parental respect opens the door to multiple unfavorable situations that can involve vocational confusion, sentimental and emotional vulnerability, detrimental procrastination in making decisions, wrong relationships and many other things that lock down a person's life and prevent opportunities.

• Premature death and bad living conditions
"Honor your father and mother, as the Lord your God commanded you. Then you will live a long, full life in the land the Lord your God is giving you" (Dt 5:16). While honoring parents brings quantitive and qualitative blessings in life, dishonoring them brings the opposite. Instead of living well and being blessed, everywhere we go, everything we do, every situation we find ourselves in will have a dark cloud hovering over it.

Worse, not only will a loss of purpose in life be their lot, many will die earlier than they would have or will suffer a life that is death-like in its nature; catatonic, paralyzed, unproductive to the point of poverty, meaningless.

CAUSE 5. Hidden sin

Hidden sin serves as an anchor that drags on the development of, and stops the dynamics of, a prosperous life: *"People who conceal their sins will not prosper, but if they confess and turn from them, they will receive mercy" (Pr 28:13)*. This not only hinders us, it prevents us from receiving both God's mercy and that of others. In turn, we are led into a state of total spiritual ruin and are deprived of God's grace.

Concealment of sin also destroys our life's structure and produces a resistance that we are not able to overcome: *"When I refused to confess my sin, my body wasted away, and I groaned all day long" (Ps 32:3)*. Life becomes extremely hard, painful and suffered in the extreme — the person remains under the judgment of sin. While a sin is buried, it is not forgiven and the person has no relief, relaxation or refreshment. Rather than experimenting mercy, he is continuously beaten up in life.

CAUSE 6. Unforgiveness and bitterness

This is extremely relevant. Satan's greatest asset against us is unforgiveness; we are unjustly wronged and feel justified to not release forgiveness for our offender. We were innocent and in the right and it is not "right" for them to simply "get off" without a penalty. It offers an inferior grace for wrongs practiced against us. It is the source of innumerous curses and torments that can legally take up residence in one's life.

In the Kingdom of God, withholding forgiveness is unforgivable. Lets consider some destructive consequences of unforgiveness.

• Poisoned emotionally

Unforgiveness opens a wound. This wound, when fed, produces bitterness. Bitterness is a spiritual toxin as poisonous as it is infectious. Unforgiveness is you taking poison but wishing for someone else to die. Obviously it is you who will end up dying. The desire for revenge is emotional suicide.

• Relationships in bondage

Forgiveness is a crucial spiritual principle. It determines whether or not we will live in liberty or bondage. The more bitterness we hold against a person, the more we take on his sin; the irony is that bitterness does not separate us from the person, it wickedly brings us closer to him through our jealousy and resentment.

Enmity (bitterness) summarizes the principle of a soul tie. We are handcuffed and bound to a person we do not forgive. We are always competing, envying and avoiding that person to such a degree that they become the center of our lives. Everything we do, or stop doing, always revolves around that person. We forfeit our peace and our freedom. We remove Jesus from the center of our lives and allow the unforgiven miscreant to take his place.

• We will not be forgiven: apostasy

"If you forgive those who sin against you, your heavenly Father will forgive you. But if you refuse to forgive others, your Father will not forgive your sins" (Mt 6:14-15). This is a text that needs to be taken very seriously. What Jesus is saying is that unforgiveness is inseparable from apostasy. This is something that we dare not ignore. Withholding forgiveness leads us into a chronic situation of disgrace, condemnation and consequently, apostasy. Apostasy is an open door to spiritual, moral and social disequilibrium. It follows a predictable cycle: rejection –> unforgiveness –> lack of grace –> apostasy –> psycho-emotional disintegration –> social corruption.

When we withhold forgiveness, we place ourselves in a situation where we will not be forgiven. This undermines our own salvation. Biblically, our salvation is conditioned on certain factors and forgiveness is one of the most important. If we cannot live with a person here on earth, we certainly cannot do so in heaven!

It is interesting to note that the main reason many people turn their backs on God, "losing their faith," is based on a framework of disappointment and bitterness. Bitterness deprives us of God's grace; the number of those who have turned from the Gospel is enormous. People who know the truth, have experienced salvation, have been recipients of God's mighty power and, because of ministerial deceptions, hurt feelings, abuse by leaders, resistance to divine correction, denominational pride, legalism, etc., have "thrown it all away" and ended up in a place of bitterness and apostasy, always feeling that they have been "wronged." The whole problem revolves around the axis of unforgiveness.

• Condemnation

"Do not judge others, and you will not be judged. For you will be treated as you treat others. The standard you use in judging is the standard by which you will be judged" (Mt 7:1-2). When we do not release forgiveness we become vulnerable to engaging in the very activity that has plagued us. Our greatest errors and failures in human interaction have the same nature as the injustices against us that we refuse to forgive. This is stated quite plainly by the apostle Paul: *"You may think you can condemn such people, but you are just as bad, and you have no excuse! When you say they are wicked and should be punished, you are condemning yourself, for you who judge others do these very same things." (Rm 2:1).*

This is very difficult to do. To illustrate, make a list of all the people who have wounded you and everything they have done against you. This will be very easy to do. Afterwards, try to list everything you have done to wound or wrong others. This will be significantly more difficult, but force yourself. There is a moment that comes when you realize that the two lists look alike. Your aggressions are a connection to the injustices you have suffered, and, instead of forgiving, you condemned, complained, threatened and even tried to get even.

The key to forgiveness is to realize that we have erred. There is no such thing as true holiness without a true commitment to practice forgiveness. The more we forgive, the less we sin. The less we forgive, the more we sin against others. If this process were not interrupted, we would end up condemned by our own standard of judgment. Physical diseases, nervous breakdowns, and emotional and depressive crises would become (or may already be) the norm in our lives.

The lack of forgiveness moves us from the seat of judgment to the prisoners' bench. Then, instead of triumph, we are condemned, imprisoned, tortured and tormented by evil spirits, people and situations.

Then the king called in the man he had forgiven and said, 'You evil servant! I forgave you that tremendous debt because you pleaded with me. Shouldn't you have mercy on your fellow servant, just as I had mercy on you?' Then the angry king sent the man to prison to be tortured until he had paid his entire debt. "That's what my heavenly Father will do to you if you refuse to forgive your brothers and sisters from your heart" (Mt 18:32-35).

Bitterness and rebellion can be defined as the hallmark — the root — of failure and injustices suffered through rejection. In short, every choice based on these attitudes will impose a framework of illness, emotional distress, mood alterations, nervous breakdowns, mental and spiritual oppression and even torture by demonic spirits.

Another principle that emphasizes this connection is the Lord's Supper. The essence of the supper is reconciliation and communion. We are urged to give ourselves an intense self-examination. Any negligence in this can be fatal.

> *"That is why you should examine yourself before eating the bread and drinking the cup. For if you eat the bread or drink the cup without honoring the body of Christ, you are eating and drinking God's judgment upon yourself. That is why many of you are weak and sick and some have even died" (1 Co 11:28-30).*

To merely practice a ritual of taking the Lord's Supper without examining our moral position can bring tragic consequences. When we take the supper without forgiving, we are sinning against the unity and the integrity of the body of Christ. As Paul noted, this is the real reason for many people being sick and even dying prematurely.

CAUSE 7. Words spoken by parents and authorities

This cause carries two situations that need to be considered:

• *Condemning words matched with disobedience*
These were the prohibitory words Joshua declared after the destruction of Jericho: *At that time Joshua invoked this curse: "May the curse of the Lord fall on anyone who tries to rebuild the town of Jericho. At the cost of his firstborn son, he will lay its foundation. At the cost of his youngest son, he will set up its gates." (Jo 6:26).*

Centuries later his words had not lost their power: *"It was during his reign that Hiel, a man from Bethel, rebuilt Jericho. When he laid its foundations, it cost him the life of his oldest son, Abiram. And when he completed it and set up its gates, it cost him the life of his young-*

est son, Segub. This all happened according to the message from the Lord concerning Jericho spoken by Joshua son of Nun" (1 Kg 16:34).

• *Abusive words giving rise to bitterness*

No father or leader has the right to curse his children or disciples. When it occurs, the victim needs be careful that he not become bitter. Bitterness produces shame, which activates a malignant prophecy over one's life. The key is to respond with brokenness, forgiveness and even prayer for the person, as Jesus strategically taught. This acts as a shield that prevents the bitterness from producing roots.

Without bitterness, malignant prophecies are annulled. If a person continues to be bitter and thus remain in a rebellious state, he is abusing his position of power or authority.

CAUSE 8. Unequally yoked

"...The men of Judah have defiled the Lord's beloved sanctuary by marrying women who worship idols. May the Lord cut off from the nation of Israel every last man who has done this..." (Ml 2:10-12)

Unequal yoking is a spiritual alliance with demons and is consolidated through cohabitation or marriage with ungodly people. The problem with marrying a person who is not a believer is the "father-in-law." If you are a child of God and the other person is the daughter of a "foreign god" spiritually, her father will become your father-in-law. This demon now is your relative. After the wedding, with what authority will you refuse a visit from your "father-in-law?" Rather than inviting God into your marriage to bless it, you will be extending an invitation to demons to "bring you Hell."

This was the transgression of Solomon (Ne 13:23-27). As Malachi asserts: *"May the Lord cut off from the nation of Israel every last man who has done this,"* the primary curse that accompanies the unequal yoking is apostasy. The Bible says that the gods of Solomon's wives corrupted his heart. This caused his heart to wander from his true love and into apostasy. The person who corrupts his values by trying to reconcile light with darkness, justice with injustice and Christ with Baal is imposing on himself a spiritual yoke of excommunication from Christ's body.

It is very important to consider four filters before marrying. It is not just a matter of the person. Are we also willing to marry their God, values, mission and family?

• Filter of the person's God – spiritual protection. Who is their "God?" Spiritually you are marrying him. He will be your new relative.

• Filter of the person's values and character – moral protection. These are the values that govern behavior. In the same manner that a person's values are corrupted, the marital relationship suffers.

• Filter of the person's mission – ministerial protection. This brings security and livelihood, affinity and fulfillment. Marrying a person who does not share your calling is a guarantee that there will be an existential crisis in your marriage.

• Filter of the person's family – generational protection. You need to understand the patterns of familial relationship and inheritance of your future spouse. Both you and your children will be influenced by the family history of our spouse.

CAUSE 9. All involvement with the occult (spiritism, witchcraft, satanism, etc.)

"For example, never sacrifice your son or daughter as a burnt offering. And do not let your people practice fortune--telling, or use sorcery, or interpret omens, or engage in witchcraft, or cast spells, or function as mediums or psychics, or call forth the spirits of the dead. Anyone who does these things is detestable to the Lord. It is because the other na-tions have done these detestable things that the Lord your God will drive them out ahead of you" (Dt 18:10-12).

"Troubles multiply for those who chase after other gods. I will not take part in their sacrifices of blood or even speak the names of their gods." (Ps 16:4).

"Well, both these things will come upon you in a mo-ment: widowhood and the loss of your children. Yes, these calamities will come upon you, despite all your witchcraft and magic." (Is 47:9)

The consequences of involvement with the occult are intense. Multiplied suffering, death of children, early widowhood, estrangement from God, destruction, death and every imaginable type of misery are the types of consequences that are associated with occult involvement.

Anything that was received from, and all involvement with, spiritism and new age practices need to be radically renounced. As we have noted earlier, it is far too common to see people in the church in strategic positions of intercession ministering with occultic gifts. Not only does this generate confusion, it sets the person up for multiple and severe consequences.

Pacts, consecration rituals, promises made to saints, spirit guides, adoration of angels, spiritual baptisms, special prayers, objects of adoration, spells, mantras, acquired supernatural capabilities, etc., all need to be specifically renounced, repented of and repudiated. It is worth reinforcing the point – we cannot sum up deliverance as a prayer that renounces something, even if it is very detailed. There must be a radical break with, and condemnation of, all involvement with witchcraft, spiritism and the new age. To do anything less is to leave yourself exposed to ongoing turmoil.

CAUSE 10. A history of necromancy
– praying and devotion to Orthodox or Catholic Saints

This is a derivative of the previous point. Praying to a saint is worshipping the dead and invoking the dead is practicing witchcraft. Every repetition of this practice throws the individual under the abominable error of necromancy, the practice of conjuring up the dead and defined as magic, sorcery and witchcraft. Although many religions sanction this practice, it is strongly forbidden by the Bible. Thinking they are invoking God, the practitioner is in fact submitting themselves to spirits of death.

The Bible explains that a mistake of this nature literally handcuffs a person to the experience of ongoing suffering and loss. They actually suffer even more than they otherwise would; they are spiritually and emotionally stoned to death, left injured, wounded and ruined: *"Men and women among you who act as mediums or who consult the spirits of the dead must be put to death by stoning. They are guilty of a capital offense." (Lv 20:27).*

CAUSE 11. Attempts at suicide
and a history of suicides in the family line

Suicide is the greatest statement of failure that a person can make. Simply stated, it is a human sacrifice; it opens a door of attack and persecution that will plague the person's offspring, an unintended consequence of what is often viewed as a selfish act. There are obvious symptoms associated with suicide, or the attempt, before it actually occurs: a strong sense of failure, withdrawal, generalized depression characterized by thoughts of suicide, chronic apathy, obsessive fear of dying or becoming sick, etc.

The majority of suicides are related to divorce. Divorce and suicide go together. Even more prevalent than adolescents who kill themselves because of destroyed homes are men aged 50 and above who are living alone. When they were younger they could fill the emotional void of a broken relationship with other women. After 50, things have changed with their older age and many of them cannot live with the anguish of rejection and loneliness.

There are three issues involved in suicide or attempted suicide that need to be addressed spiritually:

• The blood pact

The blood shed in a suicide preserves an alliance with the spirits of death, failure, impoverishment and depression. Spiritually speaking, this credit of injustice authorizes a familial persecution and subjugation that is generational. This is the reason that suicide can become cyclical in a family line. Every suicide is a renewal of a blood pact that needs to be sacerdotally repented of and confessed.

• The motivation behind the suicide

The type of spiritual oppression that attaches itself to a family's lineage is closely associated with the actual motivation behind the person killing himself. It is through the motivation and the manner the person committed suicide that this spiritual oppression burrows itself into the family lineage.

In cases of suicide it is fundamental to discover the real motivation behind the death. It is necessary to corporately and intercessorially treat the cause via confession and repentance. It does not matter what the motivations was – marital betrayal, financial bankruptcy, depression, loneliness, loss of loved ones, etc. – but it is essential to find it. It is exactly in these specific areas that the spirit of failure, impoverishment and depression will settle into the person's lineage to recreate the same pattern of despair and self-destruction.

• *The method of suicide*

It is also important to deal with the form of suicide, e.g., hanging, shooting, stabbing, poisoning, etc., in order to disconnect the influence of these death mechanisms on the offspring of the victim.

CAUSE 12. Murder and a history of murder in the lineage

Murder is the most ruthless act of anger and loss of control that humans can practice. It creates a blood pact with the spirits of death, violence and loss of control, and it brings terrible consequences over the life, family and children of the murderer.

I will never forget a police officer that I once counseled. He had been directly involved in the "disappearance" of many criminals. Strange things started to happen to him and to his family. He was involved in accidents where people died. His daughter began to suffer strange demonic possessions. He was beset with chronic afflictions and began to chronically suffer spiritual, emotional and familial violence, his finances began to fall apart. All the evidence pointed to a comprehensive attack by the spirit of destruction and death.

Because of all this, the family sought help at an evangelical church where they became members. However the daughter continued to suffer demonic attacks. The incidents only changed when the man decided to address the whole situation pastorally with his family. From that day forward his daughter never suffered another demonic attack. In this case, I am only speaking of treating the spiritual issues; the societal debt the man accumulated through his crimes is another matter that involves several factors. He is liable to arrest and could be sentenced to prison or even death.

The symptoms of murders that appear in one's lineage are covert: feelings of persecution, generalized destructive tendencies, constantly being put at risk of dying, fear and a continuous feeling of death, uncontrolled hatred to the point of wishing people's death, a tendency to commit crimes.

As with suicide, it is important to treat each murder in relation to the blood pact, the basic motivation behind it and the method of killing used in the murder.

CAUSE 13. Abortion and a history of abortions

This is an extension of the previous point. Abortion can be spiritually defined as the murdering of offspring. In addition to bringing a legacy of death, destruction and depression over one's posterity, abortion also cloisters the person in a chronic situation of sterility in various areas of life. It demonizes the uterus.

Professional, financial, spiritual, and sentimental success is always aborted in an amazingly traumatic manner. Illnesses related to the reproductive system begin to plague the person. Plans and projects begin to be chronically frustrated. Just when it is thought that something is going to work out, it unexpectedly dies. Nothing that is started is ever finished. A spirit of death prevails in everything, destroying fertility, impeding fruitfulness and preventing personal fulfillment in multiple areas of life.

(To obtain more detailed information on this topic, see chapter 4 of "*The New Wineskins Revival*" and chapter 5 of "*Roots of Depression*," both by Marcos de Souza Borges — www.editorajocum.com.br).

CAUSE 14. Thefts and robberies

The Bible is categorical in stating that greed imprisons the soul and disrupts the home (Pr 1:19). Every stolen object brings much more harm than it does good. The person thinks he is smart, but he actually is going to harvest a crop of torments. Money is always "slipping through his fingers." He never thrives, he is a slave to debt, he is always needy, and he loses more than he has stolen. The reason for his plight is that he has never appropriately addressed his sins in the area of thefts and robberies.

Then he said to me, "This scroll contains the curse that is going out over the entire land. One side of the scroll says that those who steal will be banished from the land; the other side says that those who swear falsely will be banished from the land. And this is what the Lord of Heaven's Armies says: I am sending this curse into the house of every thief and into the house of everyone who swears falsely using my name. And my curse will remain in that house and completely destroy it — even its timbers and stones." (Ze 5:3-4).

The Bible says there is a curse associated with stealing. Every person who steals, thinking he is improving his lot, will be cut off at his roots. There is an intimate connection between stealing and lying — the thief becomes a liar. A curse is released into the life of the thief and it will consume — steal — his family's material means.

More than just repentance is required when spiritually dealing with stealing. Confession and restitution, when possible, are crucial. The only way to effectively apply these principles is allowing the Holy Spirit to provide guidance and genuinely placing yourself under it.

Theft must be examined from a hereditary point of view. The moral law is clear: *'Cursed is anyone who steals property from a neighbor by moving a boundary marker.' And all the people will reply, 'Amen.' (Dt 17:27).* All activities that are associated in the narrow or broad sense of theft such as the stealing of land, enrichment through slavery (including employment abuse), illicit enrichment through social exploitation and political office, trafficking and smuggling, sexual exploitation, etc., bring a family legacy of loss through multiple generations.

Dishonest enrichment directly results in the selling out of one's family or, stated differently, theft in any form will have direct impact on the family (and descendants) of the thief. Several years ago, I read that a certain European country was supplying heroin addicts with the very heroin they were addicted to. What shocked me more was when someone told me that many of the addicts were the children of bankers who had become wealthy through the financing of drug trafficking. Quite ironically, this powerfully illustrates the power of this curse.

Another aspect of illegally acquired wealth is that in the same manner a person gains it, he will lose it. "Easy come, easy go" is very applicable here. This is especially noticeable in the case of someone becoming a believer. The devil allows the person to have wealth in order to server his own interests. Since the riches came from him, he will threaten to withdraw it, or will actually take it back, when that person considers changing, or actually does change, his values and purposes.

CAUSE 15. Sexual perversion

Sexual perversion generates a plethora of hereditary curses that destroy the family and impose such an extreme resistance that a person is often unable to remain in the church. One of the primary causes that splinters the body of Christ is related to immorality.

Writing to the Corinthians, Paul confronts them, making a direct connection between sexual perversion and an intimate, supernatural tie with demonic spirits that are involved with immorality. He further states that it is the same type of connection that we have with God: *"Don't you realize that your bodies are actually parts of Christ? Should a man take his body, which is part of Christ, and join it to a prostitute? Never!" (1 Co 6:15)*. Sexual intimacy outside of marriage creates a spiritual soul-tie, a ghoulish blood pact that joins two souls into one flesh and one soul: *"And don't you realize that if a man joins himself to a prostitute, he becomes one body with her? For the Scriptures say, 'The two are united into one'" (1 Co 6:16)*.

Therefore, it is essential that in each illicit sexual relationship (sexual partners, homosexuals, animals) there is an intentional severing of this connection between souls. Each of these perverted relationships represents spiritual handcuffs, an evil ball and chain that will be carried throughout life if not severed. This "spiritual divorce" is achieved through prayers of repentance and confession and with the assistance of spiritually mature people: *"...whatever you bind on earth will be bound in heaven, and whatever you loose on earth will be loosed in heaven" (Mt 16:19)*.

You must also pray to unravel the marital mess that was created. The person is spiritually and symbolically taken out of the role of the husband or the wife in relation to the partner of the sexual act, whether it was a human or an animal. They are purified through prayer and prophetic or spiritually symbolic acts and the purification should be extended to the conjugal bed and to the coverage of the entire family.

In some sessions where the problem of the person has a strong sexual nature, it is important to explore the history behind the loss of virginity. Especially in relation to the woman, the loss of virginity is physically a blood pact that creates the spiritual condition of "one flesh." Multiple defilements such as immorality, prostitution, abuse and violence can be established through the loss of virginity. This blood pact needs to be redeemed.

Principal sexual perversions

• Incest

Incest is sex between people of the same family, i.e., between parents and children, brothers and sisters, uncles and nephews, etc. It is important to note that incest and the spirit of abuse and violence go hand in hand. Incestuous relationships are differentiated in the Bible, as illustrated in the text below. As a means of clarifying, marriages between cousins are not included in this list.

> *"You must never have sexual relations with a close relative, for I am the Lord. Do not violate your father by having sexual relations with your mother. She is your mother; you must not have sexual relations with her. Do not have sexual relations with any of your father's wives, for this would violate your father. Do not have sexual relations with your sister or half sister, whether she is your father's daughter or your mother's daughter, whether she was born into your household or someone else's. Do not have sexual relations with your granddaughter, whether she is your son's daughter or your daughter's daughter, for this would violate yourself. Do not have sexual relations with your stepsister, the daughter of any of your father's wives, for she is your sister. Do not have sexual relations with your father's sister, for she is your father's close relative. Do not have sexual relations with your mother's sister, for she is your mother's close relative. Do not violate your uncle, your father's brother, by having sexual relations with his wife, for she is your aunt. Do not have sexual relations with your daughter-in-law; she is your son's wife, so you must not have sexual relations with her. Do not have sexual relations with your brother's wife, for this would violate your brother." (Lv 18:6-16)*

• *Prostitution*

Prostitution is when someone exchanges sex for money, goods, positions, favors, etc. Any payment or profit obtained from prostitution generationally curses the sexual and financial life of the person. Everything purchased with money from prostitution comes with a terrible dose of spiritual contamination.

> *"When you are bringing an offering to fulfill a vow, you must not bring to the house of the Lord your God any offering from the earnings of a prostitute, whether a man or a woman, for both are detestable to the Lord your God."* *(Dt 23:18)*

• *Homosexuality*

It is important to understand that homosexuality is a paradigm involving the combination of a series of factors associated with familial dysfunction and spiritual inheritances:

– Paternal orphan (no reference point regarding a father, abuse and rejection causing a chronic emotional and spiritual deficit).
– Marital role reversal (marginalization of the father and over-protection by the mother).
– Conception out of wedlock, involving fornication, adultery, incest, rape or prostitution.
– Legacy and practice of sexual perversion, bestiality and homosexuality in parents' lineage.
– Chronic adultery by one or both of the parents or hidden adulteries.
– Religious consecration and direct involvement with spiritual entities that perform the task of perverting one's sexual identity.
– Rejection of the sex of the child by parents or relatives who verbalize their frustration, harass or doubt his sexual identity. Forming expectations about the baby's sex is a delight for the spirits of homosexuality.
– Abuse or homosexual molestation in infancy.
– Homosexual molestation or abuse in childhood
– Incestuous relationships between brothers or sisters, etc.

All of this engenders a homosexual persecution which dynamically collides with the child's own will and traumatically injures his identity. Without a perspective of divine redemption, the will is defeated before it ever had a chance.

It is necessary to establish the difference between the "homosexual nature" (which does not exist) and the "homosexual character spiritual attack." This homosexual attack is often real and intense, but it can be eliminated through the appropriate mechanisms of deliverance and the re-education of sexual identity.

It is extremely important when dealing with the homosexual issue to be able to disapprove of the behavior but demonstrate acceptance of and affection for the person. Approval is conditional on motivations, principles and behaviors. The Bible condemns homosexuality but demands unconditional acceptance of the person. It links both the condemnation and the acceptance to the intrinsic value of human beings. This unconditional acceptance also holds the person accountable for the consequences of their choices while faithfully expressing the love of God; this can transform any situation and heart.

This is a critical point in the terrible conflict that the person involved in the homosexual lifestyle has to endure. We are the church and we need to love them with this love that they do not know, this love that accepts, respects, values and embraces them without prejudice and without having to take them to bed to prove it. Only the love of God can restore them to the eternal purpose of their existence!

From the perspective of the invisible world, there is no possibility of human achievement within a homosexual relationship. It is something abominable that invokes demonic forces that are relentlessly destructive. Homosexuality mutilates sexual identity, leading to the most abominable levels of corruption and destruction: *"Do not practice homosexuality, having sex with another man as with a woman. It is a detestable sin." (Lv 18:22)*

Even with all the media and governmental campaigns promoting the acceptance of the gay and lesbian lifestyle, the irony is that the more that society accepts and even approves homosexual conduct, the more the very people who all the favor is designed to protect will continue to be spiritually, emotionally and even physically rejected, abhorred, attacked and murdered. This is not merely a human question; it is an inflexible sanction of the spiritual world:

"If a man practices homosexuality, having sex with another man as with a woman, both men have committed a detestable act. They must both be put to death, for they are guilty of a capital offense." (Lv 20:13)

• Bestiality

Bestiality or zoophilia is having sex with animals. The consequent curse is confusion. In every sexual relationship there exists a sharing of identity; an immoral connection between a person and an animal is the worst kind of sexual perversion and is exploited by demons.

"A man must not defile himself by having sex with an animal. And a woman must not offer herself to a male animal to have intercourse with it. This is a perverse[1] act." (Lv 18:23)

It is very common for people who engage in bestiality to begin to assume the traits of the animal. They develop an "animal and devilish" passivity that spiritually blocks their identity, personality and behavior.

"If a woman presents herself to a male animal to have intercourse with it, she and the animal must both be put to death. You must kill both, for they are guilty of a capital offense." (Lv 20:16)

---

[1] The Hebrew term *tevel*, "perversion", derives from the verb "to mix; to confuse" and therefore refers to illegitimate mixtures of species or violation of the natural order of things.

4

THE PROCESS OF CRUCIFIXION

The dynamics of a life committed to the sacrifice of Christ

This is the most essential part of this book. Just as there is a spiritual distance between symptoms of curse and their respective causes, so there is a distance between the causes and the cross. Obviously, without the crucifixion the causes of a curse will not be subject to the cross of Christ.

According to our diagram, crucifixion can be defined as the therapeutic and redemptive ability to cover the distance between the cause of curses and the cross of Christ. It is the process of adequately interacting with the principles implicit in the sacrifice of Jesus, described below, which will trigger the benefits that will transform our life: *"All praise to God, the Father of our Lord Jesus Christ, who has blessed us with every spiritual blessing in the heavenly realms because we are united with Christ" (Ep 1:3).*

There is a spiritual differentiation between the cross and the crucifixion. The cross is a historical fact regardless of our choices. Whether we want to know or not, whether we accept it or not, Jesus died to justify us and restore our communion with the Father. The crucifixion is an intentional choice to submit to the principles proposed by Jesus in his death. It needs to be "verbalized," activated and experienced in each specific situation where sin and injustice has affected us.

The cross of Christ is God's response to the human fall, while the crucifixion is the human response to God's response. It is the validation of all that Jesus did for us. What good is the fact that Jesus paid the price of guilt for humanity if people do not know it? Having the right to salvation does not mean that you have salvation. The fact that Jesus died on the cross in our place does not automatically save everyone. It does not work that way.

In the same way, when we understand, believe and accept what Jesus did for us on the cross, we have the "right" to a life that is totally free, healthy and abundant. However, effectively enjoying this life is much more than simply having the right to it. Despite every believer having the right to a liberated life, the truth is that few actually experience it. This is the distance between the cross and the crucifixion.

The cross of Christ, i.e., the historical event of Jesus' death, only has validity when we voluntarily interact with the life it proposes.

TRANSPARENCY AND RECONCILIATION

Transparency and reconciliation should be considered the "trunk principles" from which sprout all other principles relevant to the process of crucifixion.

"But if we are living in the light, as God is in the light, then we have fellowship with each other, and the blood of Jesus, his Son, cleanses us from all sin" (1 Jo 1:7).

The basic context here is not just forgiveness, but purification. A purified life means that the person is not only pardoned, but is also free of any contamination, is healthy and subject to prosperity. The concept of spiritual purification goes well beyond being forgiven. It means that all justice has been satisfied, that all the resources of heaven have been applied to the situation, that full transparency and flexibility to repair relationships is now available and that the previous sinful state has been clarified, corrected and renewed. It eliminates all arguments to the contrary.

Note that this text starts with a conditional article: "If." It is simple and there is no middle ground. If you exercise transparency and rec-onciliation, the blood of Jesus purifies. This needs to be demystified. If you do not exercise transparency and reconciliation, no matter how much you verbally invoke the blood or the name of Jesus, it will not free you from your accumulated contamination. It remains in place and becomes the basis of Satan's arguments against you.

Neither the name of Jesus nor the blood of his sacrifice function as an amulet or magic words that can save or protect us, regardless of our relationship with God and the values He has established.

Pardon versus Purification

A person might have been forgiven and not yet purified of sins. In order to be forgiven of your sins, sincere repentance is sufficient. For purification, more is needed. If there has not been an interaction with the principles of transparency *(living in the light)* and reconciliation *(we have fellowship)*, there still exists a spiritual bottleneck and a balance of dead works that have to be reconciled. They undermine our conscience, keeping us in shackles and open to demonic exploitation. Repentance deals with the guilt of sin. Transparency and reconciliation dissolve the human and spiritual consequences. It muffles the voice of the accuser.

Satan is the prince of darkness. Spiritual ignorance, blindness and hidden sin fall under his jurisdiction. To deal with this ignorance we need God's revelation. To deal with blindness we need love and discipline, allowing others to help us see what we are not. To deal with the framework of shame, guilt and hidden sins we need the brokenness of confession. Similarly, any breaking of alliances, fraud or offenses that were not properly corrected and restitution made place us squarely under his contamination.

DEALING WITH THE WOUND OF ADULTERY

Western society has been minimizing adultery for some time. It has become increasing commonplace, especially in the context of the church. It is frightening to see the increase of "evangelicals" in the indexes marking the rise of adultery. This makes it worthwhile to illustrate the difference between forgiveness and purification and broaden our understanding of how to deal with the issue of adultery.

Suppose a husband has committed adultery, has truly repented in his heart, but still has not corrected the situation with his family. Did God pardon him? Yes. Has his marriage been purified? No. Stated differently, as long as he keeps this sin in the dark, evading the humiliation, confession and reconciliation, the marriage and the family remain at spiritual risk.

It is important to understand that marriage brings with it an identity, an awareness and a purpose. Adultery delivers a deathblow to the marriage, demonizing the person, the relationship, the marital bed and the children. It is very important to reflect on the implications of adultery, mentioned in the previous chapter, especially if you are being tempted or are considering it. Once adultery occurs, the path to a possible restoration is always very painful and traumatic.

Surgical Reconciliation

"Come, let us return to the Lord. He has torn us to pieces; now he will heal us. He has injured us; now he will bandage our wounds. In just a short time he will restore us, so that we may live in his presence. Oh, that we might know the Lord! Let us press on to know him. He will respond to us as surely as the arrival of dawn or the coming of rains in early spring." (Ho 6:1-3)

The book of Hosea deals with one of the worst phases of Israel's history. God's relationship with His people is prophetically dramatized through Hosea's marriage to a prostitute. The central context of the book is the adultery of the nation. The text above shows how God deals with this kind of moral wound. What does it mean when it says *"He has injured us; now he will bandage our wounds?"* Nothing more and nothing less than a surgical intervention. This is the therapy proposed by God to treat cancer of the nation's adultery. They would be wounded, carried into captivity in Babylon for 70 years and then restored. It would be a long therapeutic process that would surgically produce a genuine knowledge of God.

I know that many will not like what I am going to say, and will even disagree with it. Some pastors want to simplify or superficially address the situation because they think that this approach is too rigid. I have heard many people who have committed adultery say: "If I tell my spouse, my marriage will end!" Let's be honest here, the fact is that the marriage ended when adultery was committed. If there is still any chance to rescue it, it is through confession. Confession is the only surgery that can possibly remove the "cancer" that adultery produced in the marriage and the family. Often the marriage was already in a terminal state and now confession is the only thing that might save it. You should think about the consequences before committing adultery. The only solution available to you after the fact is to courageously face the trauma of surgery.

Many want deliverance, but only up to a point. When it is time to die to yourself, becoming transparent and accountable for your own sins, most people desist. The result is that we have many cases of people going through numerous "deliverances" that have not produced any benefit.

The wound produced by adultery becomes so internalized that it demands surgical intervention. There is no way to resolve or confess adultery without the betrayed spouse, and consequently the marriage itself, being traumatically wounded. No one is ever prepared to hear that their spouse has betrayed them. They experience a true passing through the valley of the shadow of death. But regardless of how painful it is, this is the prescription, the medicine of the cross. If there is any chance of saving the marriage, this is the path. Oddly enough, in my experience of mediating this type of confession on multiple occasions, I have never seen it fail.

It begins with a sincere confession and is sustained by a legitimate commitment to change. Next comes the process of the betrayed party forgiving their spouse. An even more difficult process can be the betrayed spouse's forgiving the person with whom their guilty spouse betrayed them (in cases involving relatives and friends this can be extremely traumatic). Finally, the most difficult process is rebuilding lost confidence. Compared to this ultimate challenge, forgiveness seems easy.

THE DAVID – BATHSHEBA CASE

Let's look at a classic situation of adultery, the famous case of David and Bathsheba – a deliverance in the style of the prophet Nathan.

"This is what the Lord says: Because of what you have done, I will cause your own household to rebel against you. I will give your wives to another man before your very eyes, and he will go to bed with them in public view. You did it secretly, but I will make this happen to you openly in the sight of all Israel" (2 Sm 12:11-12).

Adultery is one of the greatest disgraces that a person can commit in life. It is difficult for any other sin to collectively bring as much pain, suffering, destruction and disruption as adultery. It should be helpful to examine some insights and steps that we need to take to deal with these situations.

The latent power of hidden adultery

• Typically, people who commit adultery go to terrible extremes in an attempt to conceal it. They begin to live a life based on a lie. David went as far as to kill for it. After several attempts to make it appear that the child was Uriah's, David decided to kill him. Uriah was one of his most loyal men but David strategically and premeditatedly killed him using his general to do his dirty work.

• Attempts to conceal adultery create a wasting of the soul that is unbearable: *"When I refused to confess my sin, my body wasted away, and I groaned all day long. Day and night your hand of discipline was heavy on me. My strength evaporated like water in the summer heat" (Ps 32:3-4)*. The person's spiritual life begins to chronically waste away and this can enable new relapses, sinful desires and can actually lead to their complete destruction.

• Sooner or later, the truth will come out. It is a ticking time bomb. Jesus made it clear that there is no escape: *"Whatever you have said in the dark will be heard in the light, and what you have whispered behind closed doors will be shouted from the housetops for all to hear!" (Lk 12:2-3)*. There are two ways of dealing with adultery, both of which can produce different consequences:

– Expose yourself. Anticipate the scandal, acting with humility, brokenness and love to God's discipline. In a certain way, this leaves us in control of the situation.

– Be exposed. This is terrifying. The more we try to hide adultery, the more vulnerable we become. This is the active principle for constructing a scandal, where we lose all control of the situation and are thrown under the bus of the family, ministry, church ...

• When we harden our heart and stop listening to the Holy Spirit, God brings in a prophet. This is what happened Nathan confronted David (2 Sm 12). When discovered, we need to become humble. Maybe there is hope. Choose to deny it, deflect it, put a different spin on it and you are committing suicide. The humiliation David experienced when confronted by Nathan was vital. In cases of adultery, wise mediation can make all the difference. This text illustrates a powerful and effective deliverance conducted in a wise and prophetic manner as Nathan is led to confront, treat and establish the punishment that would fall on the House of David.

• Sooner or later, this sin will find you out, causing incredible damage to family relationships. *"...I will cause your own household to rebel against you..."* Betrayal is implicit in adultery. It is associated with the closest relationships. A stranger cannot betray you; the most that can happen is that you are deceived. Adultery releases an unimaginable process of treason, disappointment and loss with the people we love the most and from whom we would least expect it.

The family of David was ruined. His first son with Bathsheba died, Ammon raped Tamar, Absalom avenged Tamar by coldly murdering Ammon at a family dinner, taking justice into his own hands. As a result, a deep bitterness was established between David and Absalom, who after rebelling against his father, was murdered by Joab, David's nephew and the head of his army ...a literal trail of death and destruction.

• What parents do in the dark, their children will do in the light. The worst type of punishment is to see our hidden sins openly playing out in the lives of our children and destroying them.

Though not a hard and fast rule, it is often the case that a child's rebellion is nothing more than the side effect of a parent's hidden sin: *"...I will cause your own household to rebel against you. I will give your wives to another man before your very eyes, and he will go to bed with them in public view. You did it secretly, but I will make this happen to you openly in the sight of all Israel"* (2 Sm 12:11-12). What David did secretly, his son Absalom did in the light of day. The spirit of betrayal that led David into adultery attacked him through Absalom. He openly lies down with his father's concubines, demonstrating the intention to kill David and usurp his Kingdom.

Confronting the consequences of adultery

1. Reputation Test: Act with full transparency

When confronted by the prophet Nathan, David ripped his garments and his heart. He humbled himself. Only here, after more than a year, did his restoration begin. Reinforcing what we have already said, adultery is a type of sin that produces such an internal wound that it can only be cut out surgically. I know that this type of situation is very delicate. It is the type of "surgical reconciliation" that demands wise intermediation and much patience and fidelity if there is to be total healing.

There is no way for one spouse to confess adultery to the other without hurting them deeply. However, this is the wound that treats the wound and, unfortunately, many internal injuries can only be treated surgically. It is necessary to open, cut, tear and bleed. As painful the wound made by the surgeon may be, it is necessary and therapeutic. This is the power of transparency.

2. Position Test: Leave the Palace

It is necessary to step down off your pedestal and relinquish what has been gained. You will have to forfeit achievements and position for God. In these moments, holding onto them means becoming doubly rejected by God. David had to go through this test in order to be healed.

People who find themselves in a position of authority or government in the church must be willing to give up everything. It may seem strange, but this is the only way to save their life. David, humbly, barefoot and with the few followers who remained, abandoned the throne and the palace. He left it all behind: his kingship, his prestige, his titles and sought refuge in dependence on God. Had he stayed at the palace, his own son who demonstrated this intention by openly laying with his father's concubines would surely have murdered him.

3. The Shimei Test: Experiencing
and enduring the time of stoning

For David, the stoning became literal when, leaving the palace, he had to face Shimei: *"So David and his men continued down the road, and Shimei kept pace with them on a nearby hillside, cursing as he went and throwing stones at David and tossing dust into the air. (2 Sm 16:13)"*

David knew that his sin from prior years had found him. He had been warned of this. David was the issue here, not Absalom or Shimei. He understood what was happening, bowing his head and bearing his stoning without retaliation.

"Why should this dead dog curse my lord the king?" Abishai *son of Zeruiah demanded. "Let me go over and cut off his head!" "No!" the king said. "Who asked your opinion, you sons of Zeruiah! If the Lord has told him to curse me, who are you to stop him?" (2 Sm 16:9-10).* Incredibly, David did not say that Satan was using Shimei, but that God himself was behind it. What discernment! It was only at this moment that he received God's purification and things began to revert back to his favor.

People who have committed adultery need to be prepared to confront the "Shimeis." Shimei represents all the verbal, spiritual, conjugal, familial, social and ministerial aggression that comes with the consequences of adultery. It is necessary to bear it silently. This is not an "attack of the devil," it is a test of God. David had to go through the Shimei test.

Whoever commits adultery must understand that many are going to slander, curse, condemn, attack, etc. Now they must bear it silently, without retaliation. This is the time of stoning. I am sorry to have to say this, but it is what is really going to happen. The majority of those who go through this test fail and exit the necessary path of brokenness.

4. The Absalom Test: Experiencing
the result of our own betrayal and rebellion
Everyone who betrays someone will drink the same poison. David had to go through the Absalom test. How we deal with this determines the direction of our life. Bitterness destroys us but brokenness restores us. After humiliating himself before Shimei, David interceded for Absalom.

We have to experience the consequences of our own rebellion and infidelity through the people we love the most and who are the most precious to us.

Once more David did not fight against flesh and blood. Absalom represents those people who are like children to us, who are wounded, who have issues that have not been resolved and are potentially vulnerable to betrayal. They are like nitroglycerine that is being shaken. It is the betrayal of adultery that comes against the perpetrator exponentially. The focus is not Absalom's rebellion but David's adultery. Having to deal with the "Absalom situation" is much more difficult that the "Shimei issue." Your child will never stop being your child. David tried everything to save Absalom's life but failed to do so.

After all of this, experiencing the result of his sin, his punishment, quietly bearing all correction and insult, being condemned in all of his actions, David had his throne restored and was still recognized by God as a man after His own heart. This is the power of complete brokenness that glorifies the cross of Christ. God continues to have a plan for everyone who exits the plan!

HITTING THE TARGET
Redemptive principles implicit in the sacrifice of Jesus

The crucifixion may be succinctly defined as the process of denying yourself. Its essence is the exercise of full transparency and being open to reconciling and reeducating our ability to relate to others. I would like to review the various parameters of the crucifixion. These are the "weapons of blood;" *"they have defeated him by the blood of the Lamb..." (Re 12:11).*

PRINCIPLE 1. Humiliation

This is the process of renouncing our reputation in order to responsibly address the sins, wounds, injustices and frauds we commit or suffer. This is the most penetrating point of the conflict. Pride tries to impose itself in various manners: from one extreme of a subtle and plausible pretext to evade responsibility to the other extreme of aggressive rebellion against it. We generate a plethora of arguments and sophistries in our minds that almost create a convincing justification that allows us to deflect the necessity of traveling this undesirable path. The voice of self-righteousness, bitterness and shame become increasingly demanding in order to enforce an unhealthy stubbornness to not submit to the process.

However, this conflict between humiliation and reputation is decisive. Humiliation has to speak louder than reputation.

"The high and lofty one who lives in eternity, the Holy One, says this: 'I live in the high and holy place with those whose spirits are contrite and humble. I restore the crushed spirit of the humble and revive the courage of those with repentant hearts'" (Is 57:15).

The indwelling of God and the visitation of God are two different experiences. Isaiah mentions two places where the presence of God dwells: either on the high and holy throne or in a contrite and humble heart. There is no middle ground; either He lives in the heights of His majesty or He intensely inhabits the depths of a broken and humble heart: *"The Lord is close to the brokenhearted; he rescues those whose spirits are crushed"* (Ps 34:18).

Humiliation is the flagship for the healing of the land: *"If my people who are called by my name will humble themselves and pray and seek my face and turn from their wicked ways, I will hear from heaven and will forgive their sins and restore their land"* (2 Ch 7:14).

The largest barrier in the path of deliverance is pride, idolatry of honor and the love of reputation. Without removing this initial resistance of the soul, we place ourselves squarely on the road away from our freedom.

PRINCIPLE 2. Confession

This is the process of revealing your sin(s), guilt and shame in a personal or intercessory manner to both God and others. This produces an instant impact. This is when light dissipates darkness, truth undoes the lie, brokenness opens the prisons of the soul, angels defeat demons and the cross trumps curses, communicating God's miracles and purifying the whole spiritual atmosphere.

"Confess your sins to each other and pray for each other so that you may be healed. The earnest prayer of a righteous person has great power and produces wonderful results." (Ja 5:16)

To confess is to spiritually expose sin to the light of God. It is important to understand that God Himself, upon judging Lucifer and the angels who followed him in his rebellion, sentenced them to live in darkness. Jesus refers to Satan as being the Prince of Darkness.

The sphere of action delegated by God to the devil is not limited to the fact that the person is a Christian, has a religion, believes in God or belongs to a church, or not. The jurisdiction (*topos*), i.e. the environment in which Satan has power, is restricted to the darkness. Where there are areas of darkness, obscurity, deceit, concealment, blindness or ignorance in the life of any person, this is their *habitat*, their sphere of influence, oppression, obsession and even possession. This is Satan's legacy: to build his world of darkness in the darkness of the human soul and to make it hell.

Therefore it is easy to conclude that demonic entities feed on our silence, our quiet guilt, our secret sins, our implicit shame in moral passivity, our emotional muzzles and our spiritual timidity. The domination exercised by demonic strongholds is directly proportional to our spiritual resistance to confess indomitable guilt or shame.

Whether we like it or not, everything that is in darkness is subject to a direct intervention of Satan. However, when our confession is more scandalous than our sin and we have decided to be spiritually bold by crucifying our reputation and judging ourselves, we will not be condemned with the world. The Bible guarantees that we will experience the faithfulness and righteousness of God that is revealed in the perfect sacrifice of Jesus.

PRINCIPLE 3. Repentance

Repentance is not the conviction of sin. The conviction of sin is a part of the process of repentance, but it is not repentance. Repentance is also not confession. Confession is simply another extremely important step in the direction of repentance. Do not fool yourself by just taking these first two steps.

Repentance is birthed by the decision to change! As you probably already know, the Greek word for repentance is *metanóia*. It means a change of mind, motivation and purpose. It indicates that the person has decided to travel in an opposite direction from that which he was traveling. Repentance is not simply being convicted or confessing; it is a change, a radical transformation of both motivation and behavior. The concept demands a posturing or positioning that is crucial. Repentance is not a process; it is an internal and irreversible decision to align ourselves with the will of God in relation to our mistakes and sins.

> *"People who conceal their sins will not prosper, but if they confess and turn from them, they will receive mercy"* *(Pr 28:13).*

This text shows the crucial detail involved in repentance: "...and turn from." Repentance occurs when, in addition to not covering up our sin, we confess it and make the irrevocable decision to leave it. As Jesus said to the adulterous woman who was almost stoned to death: *"...Neither do I [condemn you]. Go and sin no more" (Jo 8:11).* Repentance awakens the power to change. This was not a threat but a recommendation saturated with grace and the power to change.

Crossing the Jordan – The baptism of repentance

Repentance is allegorized in Joshua 3. I would advise you that before you continue here, go read this chapter in your Bible. The central subject of the chapter is the crossing of the Jordan River. The crossing alludes to the baptism of repentance, i.e., a change, a watershed, a breakpoint. The Jordan separated the desert from the land of Canaan; spiritually, a separation of a mediocre life of drought in the desert from an abundant life of achievement and conquest in Canaan.

Which side do you want to live on? This is the power of repentance. It is when you stop living on manna, spiritual milk, and begin to live off of the innovations of the land, learning how to sow and reap the purpose of God. Lets look at some important aspects of repentance:

• Be focused on the alliance
"When you see the Levitical priests carrying the Ark of the Covenant of the Lord your God, move out from your positions and follow them" (vs. 3). Salvation is based on preserving our alliance with God. This requires a style of life based on repentance and performance. Repentance is the ingredient of the Supper that

leads us to renew our covenant with God, in Christ, preserving our communion with Him. *"So anyone who eats this bread or drinks this cup of the Lord unworthily is guilty of sinning against the body and blood of the Lord. That is why you should examine yourself before eating the bread and drinking the cup" (1 Co 11:27-28).* The frame of reference of the spiritual life is the alliance.

• Be aware of the Holy Spirit

"...Stay about a half mile behind them" (vs. 4). It is essential to give space to the Holy Spirit to work. The "half-mile" is the distance that the Holy Spirit needs in our hearts for us to know to choose the right direction. We resist Him when we get too close to the ark through spiritual pride or we fall too far behind by allowing our hearts to become hard. We need to give to the Spirit the right distance so He can convict us of sin, of righteousness and of judgment. This matures the irrevocable decision to change that is implicit in genuine repentance.

• Plan the decision to change

"Then Joshua told the people, 'Purify yourselves, for tomorrow the Lord will do great wonders among you'" (vs. 5). Repentance requires a psychological preparation and mental planning. Sin is seductive, captivating and addictive. It is not easy to break an addiction or the severity imposed by the practice or compulsion of sin. It is necessary to take a breath, psychologically speaking, so we can allow the decision the Holy Spirit is leading us to take to mature. Do everything necessary to not turn back. The basis of sanctification is our will being inclined towards the will of God; this allows Him to supernaturally operate in our life.

• Hope in the complete victory

"Today you will know that the living God is among you. He will surely drive out the Canaanites, Hittites, Hivites, Perizzites, Girgashites, Amorites, and Jebusites ahead of you" (vs. 10). God is committed to honoring our decision to change. His supernatural intervention that happens when repenting is the guarantee that sin will not have dominion over us. Every enemy of our soul will be defeated.

- *Take the step of faith, obedience and the miracle of change*
"The priests will carry the Ark of the Lord, the Lord of all the earth. As soon as their feet touch the water, the flow of water will be cut off upstream, and the river will stand up like a wall" (vs. 13). This is the divine aspect of repentance. When we are inspired by our priestly calling and by our obedience to our covenant with God, to confront the sin that separates us from a life of victory, we will experience the supernatural power of God.

Repentance occurs when we irrevocably decide to abandon a sin. It is when we resist the sin to the point of shedding blood *("resisted unto blood" – KJV)*, as the Hebrews write exhorts (He 12:4). It is when we state to ourselves: **Even if I have to sweat blood, I will not do this again! I simply will not do it anymore!!!** We decide to put an end to spiritual disarray. This is the point where grace and the supernatural power of God reach us. The waters of the Jordon separate and a road that we have never traveled opens up. We have an unforgettable experience, a superhuman deliverance that changes the direction of our soul. As Paul testifies: it is when God operates in both our desire and our action. He completes the work that was started with our willingness to change!

At this point it is no longer us that leaves the sin, it is the sin that leaves us! The fear of the Lord begins to dominate this area of our soul. We begin to have the same repugnance that God has in relation to the sin. His grace allows us to overcome. Grace is not permission to sin: to the contrary, it is the manifest power of God that empowers us to defeat the sin that has enslaved us. That which was previously difficult to overcome becomes easy. This is the supernatural power of repentance! God rips out the hardened heart of our soul and gives us a new one that desires to keep his commandments. Repentance is what puts us in Canaan, the promised land, and gives us a lifetime of conquests.

PRINCIPLE 4: Forgiveness

Without forgiving we cannot be forgiven. Forgiveness is the process of responsibly confronting our wounds and resentments. Forgiveness is not a feeling — it is a commandment. It does not simply appear out of nowhere; rather, it is the result of a persistent process of choosing the way of the cross. It is only because of the cross that we can use the same words that Jesus used with his executioners: *"Father, forgive them for they know not what they do."* Lets look at some important principles about forgiveness:[1]

• Forgiveness is not a feeling, it is a choice
You will never "feel like forgiving" someone who deceived you, humiliated you, abused you, betrayed you, etc. What you will "feel" like is "strangling" him! The immediate tendency is to seek some form of revenge. However, in order to forgive, it is necessary for our own feelings and resentments to be put to death. We must deny ourselves.

• Forgiveness is not a suggestion, it is a command
Jesus established forgiveness as an uncompromising law. When Peter asked about how to forgive, Jesus made it clear that forgiveness must be a way of life, i.e., we must forgive not just seven times but seventy times seven times per day. This is the spiritual mathematics of the Kingdom of God. Forgiveness must become a lifestyle.

• Forgiveness is unilateral
Forgiveness is not based on the worthiness of the offender; it is independent of their current or past conduct. It doesn't matter if they have repented or not, if they have recognized their mistake or not, or if they have asked us for forgiveness or not. We must forgive, because this is the only way we can ensure our own emotional health and spiritual protection. Otherwise, bitterness will take root, causing serious disruption in our lives.

• To forgive does not signify forgetting
Forgiving is not forgetting; rather, it is no longer used as an argument against the person, even though you remember what

---

[1] Marcos de Souza Borges, Raízes da Depressão: Enfrentando o Grande Mal do Século (Roots of Depression: Confronting the Great Evil of the Century), Chapter 3 – "The Lack of Forgiveness and the Root of Bitterness," Editora Jocum Brasil.

happened. We need to understand the process of wound healing; the person who is healed doesn't forget what they suffered, they are able to comfortably remember it.

• To forgive someone does not mean you pretend you are not hurt
If this is the case, we must be honest with ourselves and with God and recognize that the wound exists; otherwise we will effectively boycott the relationship. Do not ignore the help that God offers. Accepting His help will prevent a wound from developing and producing bitterness.

• To forgive does not obligate us to create a friendship
This is a question that leaves many people in conflict. Does forgiving someone mean I am obligated to become a friend to that person? Forgiveness is unconditional; friendship and intimacy depend on integrity and credibility. There are requirements that determine whether we can expose ourselves to a legitimate friendship.
We cannot choose whom we will or will not forgive, but we can and should choose who is going to be a friend. However, the fact that we do not choose someone as a friend means neither that we reject a relationship with this person nor have him as an enemy. It is a thin line.

Phases of Forgiveness
It is essential to understand the process of forgiveness. This understanding can be decisive in the internal battle that an injured person must face.

• Indifference
Indifference may be the primary characteristic of an injured person. In reality, the extreme opposite of love is not hate but indifference. Prolonged rejection can produce a suffering so acute that it can destroy all feelings and annihilate any consideration for the aggressor. After fighting against rejection for extended periods of time, the tendency is to become indifferent. Since we can't literally kill the person, we choose to execute him internally in our heart.

• Anger

Realizing that we have no alternative but to forgive, the tendency is for indifference to turn into anger. This is the signal that the wound is being suppressed. As incredible as it may seem, indifference is actually worse than anger. Anger indicates that the person is reacting and beginning to come out of the emotional coma.

• Conflict

Through the conviction of the Holy Spirit, anger begins to lose its power and the person is able to begin dealing with their emotions. He realizes that he can face the hurt, but at the same time, he seems to not want to do it. A strong feeling that the offender does not deserve to be forgiven arises. However, it is no longer an unequal struggle. Knowing that he needs to forgive, he starts realizing that he can forgive. Rationally, he is able to consider that this is the best choice to make.

• Frustration

At this stage the person is totally convinced that he needs to forgive in spite of not liking the idea. There is a sense of sadness and frustration. However, at the same time that he is feeling impotent in the face of all that he has suffered, he is now fortified by a conviction that he is doing the right thing.

• Acceptance

The person conforms to the idea, putting his obedience above his feelings. His emotional life rebalances, submitted to the governance of the Spirit.

• Peace

After successfully moving into a posture of forgiveness, the person begins to enjoy a sense of peace that has eluded him for so long. This is an unquestionable sign of victory over bitterness.

• Scarred Memory

Consequently, he feels totally consoled by the Spirit of God. He can comfortably remember the injustices suffered. Though a scar can cause one to remember what happened, it does not hurt nor does it bother you. The truth is, it is proof of triumph, as Paul said: *"...for I bear on my body the scars that show I belong to Jesus" (Gl 6:17).*

• Humorous outlook

The symptom of a memory that has been cured is good humor in relation to what has been experienced. Some get to the point that they can even make jokes about the situation. A humorous outlook is, simply stated, the shortest distance between two people.

Every relationship involves risks. We are always vulnerable to big disappointments, rejections and betrayals. Anyone can be wounded. Jesus himself was wounded:

"He came to his own people, and even they rejected him" (Jn 1:11).

Those who he intentionally loved harshly rejected Jesus. The question is how we react. Your reaction is what makes all the difference in your life and in the world.

We must learn to deal with these relationship burdens and unfair situations that we have already suffered and will continue to suffer. It does not matter what has happened to us. What is important is what we are doing with what has been done to us. This will determine our character and our emotional health. Nobody can hurt us without our consent. This is the great paradigm of forgiveness. To forgive, we must deny ourselves and embrace the lifestyle demonstrated by the cross of Christ.

PRINCIPLE 5. Surrender

Capitulation is a public repudiation of all involvement in and compromises with the kingdom of darkness. It is inspired by the sacrifice and the name of Jesus. It is based on the biblical principle of what we agree with on the earth is accomplished in heaven and what we bind on earth is bound in heaven (Mt 16:19).

This process complements repentance and confession in the sense of denying the unfruitful works of darkness, breaking and annulling pacts, alliances, agreements, requests, prayers, beliefs and other understandings in relation to demonic entities. Obviously, this is not simply a long prayer of renunciation, but an active part of the deliverance process that wields and breaks power.

PRINCIPLE 6. Restitution

Restitution is the process of retracting, returning and restoring that which we damaged, stole or took from someone. While this obviously applies to material things, it is also applicable in emotional, sentimental, moral and conjugal issues as well. This is the most profound and restorative aspect of deliverance.

In regards to restitution, hidden sin (in the realm of our thoughts) should be confessed privately to God; personal sin is confessed personally to the person who was injured; public sin is to be confessed publically. This is the most powerful and effective weapon we have to free the conscience. Restitution is the most difficult principle to practice because it hurts the most. Yet, it is the most powerful in resolving things and entirely freeing us.

> *"Meanwhile, Zacchaeus stood before the Lord and said, 'I will give half my wealth to the poor, Lord, and if I have cheated people on their taxes, I will give them back four times as much!' Jesus responded, 'Salvation has come to this home today, for this man has shown himself to be a true son of Abraham'"* (Lk 19:8-9).

Here are some practical advice and practices concerning restitution:

How to make restitution

When you have harmed someone, recognition of what you have done and repentance of it are essential. Repentance will be demonstrated by asking forgiveness of the offended person (Lk 15:17-21; Dt 18:21). In the case of loss (theft, destruction, fraud, etc.), repentance will be shown by the restitution of what was stolen or taken, even if it is no longer possible to make full restitution (Nm 5:6-7; Ez 23:14-16).

Excuses for not making restitution
- It's going to cost me everything I own
- It's going to cost me what I do not have
- But it was such a small thing
- I'll make things right when...
- I wasn't the only one involved
- Things have already improved between us
- The person isn't going to understand
- The person has moved
- It happened a long time ago
- I've determined that it will never happen again
- The religious excuse: "I'm a new creature."

Wrong ways to make restitution
- Excuse me for anything I might have done
- I didn't mean to
- I made a mistake, but so did you...
- If I was wrong forgive me
- I'm sorry

How to cauterize the conscience
- Continue in the error: the more we insist on walking in sin, the more we lose spiritual sensitivity.
- Compulsive escape: alcoholism, drugs, food, fun, hard work, sleep.
- Perversion: act with passivity, going to extremes to do something that we know that we should not do, especially in the sexual area. Some people cross some lines that make it increasingly difficult for them to have a return path.
- Compensation: attempting to remove the blame by being extremely helpful, praying a lot, doing good works, etc.
- Self-deception: justify yourself by deflecting blame to facts, situations or people, or by pointing out the error of others.

Practical steps to make restitution
- Ask the Holy Spirit to reveal our heart.
- Define exactly what we need to restore or return.
- Ask for wisdom to not make the situation worse or to blame others.

• Identify the basic motive because we sometimes try to repay small things and pass over the real motive
• Be prepared to fix everything, whatever the cost. We will be surprised at how much good this causes.

Coming to Christ is not escaping the problems but solving them. You become responsible for your acts and attitudes. God is just and will not require anything that we are not able to do. The Lord will sustain us to the degree that we are being honest and responsible.

PRINCIPLE 7. Reconciliation

Reconciliation is the process of personally or intercessorially dismantling personal, generational, racial or territorial barriers. It can encompass all of these aspects with the objective of cutting the roots of any enmity, whether it is bitterness, resentment, hate, revenge, prejudice or any other demonic stronghold.

How is an evil stronghold established?[2] Imagine a conversation between a principality and a demon; remember that their objective is to destroy relationships and aggravate the Spirit of God. Here is the advice the demon might receive:

• Use a little bit of truth.
• Polarize everybody on different sides of the truth.
• Tempt them to be unfair in their calculations about each other.
• Pay special attention when they start attacking each other with rejection, harsh words and biases.
• Once they are isolated from each other and feeling guilty about what they did and said, begin to condemn them, accusing and tormenting them with remorse. Recruit other demons to help.
• Push yourself to set up a permanent stranglehold.
• While they are in pain and confused, offer them a way out through a camouflaged miscalculation, a bit of sophistry, a new teaching that obscures guilt, blame nature, facts or society. They cannot live without hope, so give them a bit of false hope for good measure.

---

[2] John Dawson, Reconciliação – Curando as Feridas das Nações (Reconciliation – Healing the Wounds of the Nations), Editora Jocum Brasil.

- Make sure that you permanently shut the prison door! Slander their understanding of God's character. Above all, blame God for what happened!

It is that simple and has been happening since Adam and Eve. Satan's methods never change (they do not have to!). The majority of the authority that Satan's kingdom has obtained has come through the partnership of accusation and deception. Our vulnerability is unresolved guilt and broken relationships.

This brings us back to the unique role of God's people – we are to exercise the ministry of reconciliation. We can only promote reconciliation by being free ourselves to exercise impartiality and honesty. We are reconciled with God through sincere confession and we help reconcile others in the same manner.

PRINCIPLE 8. Discipline and obedience (Reeducation)

Obedience inspired by God is highly restorative. The heart of obedience is discipline based on the fear of God. To fear God is to love what He loves and hate what He hates. Discipline is the process of exercising the choice to build a character of obedience. Sustaining achieved conquest is an essential part of the process of deliverance: *"And after you have become fully obedient, we will punish everyone who remains disobedient" (2 Co 10:6).*

Nothing is lasting without discipline and perseverance. This is the genuine seal of deliverance. Without this stamp, the enemy can retake the territory and the second state becomes even worse than the first.

It is important to clarify that in the fight against sin there will be some failures. This is part of the learning process and achievement. However, it is important to not place an over valued importance neither on the victories nor on the defeats. This can respectively produce neglect and abandonment. Learn to recognize achievements that come in the grace of God; learn to enjoy the benefit in the failures of being able to forgive ourselves as God forgives us. This is a legitimate inspiration of discipline that builds a character of obedience. This is the mighty virtue of patience, which can be defined as the ability to not require an immediate change from others (or ourselves). This is the only way that we can find the path of a relationship with divine grace. With this motivation discipline is sound and redemptive.

With this we can experience the power of the Law of immunity: *"From six disasters he will rescue you; even in the seventh, he will keep you from evil" (Jb 5:19).* There is a limit to the influence of evil and sin. The strength of sin can be broken when we position ourselves properly.

The number "six" in the Bible reflects imperfections and human limitations. Job explains: *"From six disasters he will rescue you…"* i.e., it is the one time that we resist and persist within our limitations, but trusting that there will come a seventh time when, by God's grace, we will overcome evil. This immunity is the synergy of the grace of God and our perseverance.

"Seven" is known as the number of totality or the perfection of completeness. Suddenly, that which has continuously defeated us from the beginning, now, after a complete process of perseverance and confidence, becomes easily surmountable. We were immune! This characterizes a real encounter with the fear of the Lord.

Discipline places us on the path to becoming strong. This is not a privilege for some; it is a choice that we can all make. The Bible exhorts us: *"when I am weak, then I am strong" (2 Co 12:10).* God said to Joshua: "Be strong and courageous." Moral force is a matter of choice. This is independent of the law of inheritance or of influences that oppress us. Faith is a muscle that needs to be continuously exercised. Discipline is faith being exercised; it is the solid possibility of human and spiritual victory!

PRINCIPLE 9. Rest

Rest is highly redemptive and consolidates each conquest we have won and each achievement we have attained. It comes as a result of genuine surrender and complete trust in the grace of God. The whole structure of resistance to God collapses in its presence. This is the powerful relationship that exists between the cross and rest. The soul begins to flow in the dynamics of peace.

Peace is an absolute security in God, even in the midst the worst and most punishing adversity. It is that supernatural place that David found in battles: *"Though a thousand fall at your side, though ten thousand are dying around you, these evils will not touch you" (Ps 91:7).* Peace eliminates any advantage the enemy has over us. The enemy loses his voice and in turn his ability to accuse, condemn or disturb us. The agony ends. This is one of the primary marks of true deliverance.

The lack of rest is a symptom of anxiety, fear, guilt, shame and any other toxin that oppresses and overloads the soul. Without confronting these with rest, the torment speaks louder than peace. We lose the blessing! This is how we invert the spirit of service. Ministry needs to be the result of our rest in God, not what comes from our stress and worry.

God is not moved by our bouts of anxiety. He does not allow Himself to be manipulated by our tantrums, fastidiousness and grumbling. Isaiah tells us that He works for those who wait for Him (Is 64:4).

While you wait, God works, and while you work, God waits. Rest is one of the great paradoxes of the cross and one of the greatest secrets of a spiritual life that is healthy and growing.

PRINCIPLE 10. Intercession

Intercession is the priestly process of representing another person (or group), inspired by God's compassion, feeling their pain, identifying with their sins and miseries, offering in their place confession, repentance, reconciliation and prayer before God, thus spiritually protecting them, their family and descendants.

> *"Every high priest is a man chosen to represent other people in their dealings with God. He presents their gifts to God and offers sacrifices for their sins. And he is able to deal gently with ignorant and wayward people because he himself is subject to the same weaknesses" (He 5:1-2).*

In fact, all the principles implicit in the previously mentioned crucifixion may be practiced intercessorially on behalf of a person who is impeded by, or imprisoned in, their ignorance, bitterness or any other type of spiritual bondage.

The 4 levels of intercession

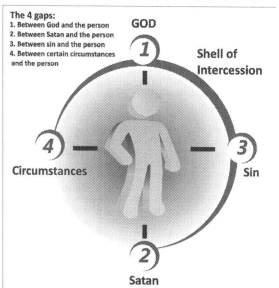

The 4 gaps:
1. Between God and the person
2. Between Satan and the person
3. Between sin and the person
4. Between certain circumstances and the person

GOD

1

Shell of Intercession

4

Circumstances

3

Sin

2

Satan

"I looked for someone who might rebuild the wall of righteousness that guards the land. I searched for someone to stand in the gap in the wall so I wouldn't have to destroy the land, but I found no one" (Ez 22:30).

The intercessor can and should place himself in the gap:

1. Between God and the person
Bring God to the person and take the person to God through prayer, evangelism, service, mercy, etc.

2. Between Satan and the person
We can also put ourselves between a person and a demonic attack, shielding them. This was what Jesus did for Peter when he attempted to persuade Jesus to not surrender to death: *"But Peter took him aside and began to reprimand him for saying such things. 'Heaven forbid, Lord,' he said. 'This will never happen to you!'" (Mt 16:22).* Jesus not only understood the subtle infiltration of Satan in the suggestion of Peter, but he also intercepted it. He protects Peter in that crucial moment against what would inevitably happen: *"Jesus turned to Peter and said, 'Get away from me, Satan! You are a dangerous trap to me. You are seeing things merely from a human point of view, not from God's'" (Mt 16:23).*

In this same context, a little later, the situation would return to repeat itself: *"Simon, Simon, Satan has asked to sift each of you like wheat. But I have pleaded in prayer for you, Simon, that your faith should not fail. So when you have repented and turned to me again, strengthen your brothers" (Lk 22:31-32).* Peter once again opens himself up to demonic speculation: *"Peter said, 'Lord, I am ready to go to prison with you, and even to die with you.' But Jesus said, 'Peter, let me tell you something. Before the rooster crows tomorrow morning, you will deny three times that you even know me'" (Lk 22:33-34).* The ending was not worse only because of Jesus' intercession. Even though he had denied Jesus, Peter was eventually restored and would go on to exercise an apostolic role that would advance the spread of the first century church.

3. Between sin and the person

This is the highest calling of the priest: to be able to identify with a person at that level where his sins are confessed. This is the same thing that Jesus did when he assumed our sins on the cross, interceding for the human race. The same principle applies to us, enabling us to intercessorially confess someone else's sins. This is especially true as we intercede on behalf of our family, lineage, church, city, nation, etc. Each member of the body of Christ is a priest with this calling.

Intercession permits us to corporately identify with the sins of someone else, experiencing God's pain in the situation and triggering the ministry of the Holy Spirit in their favor. This is what Job did for his children and what some prophets and restorers of Israel like Nehemiah, Ezra and Daniel did. They stepped in front of their ancestors and their sins due to the exile of the nation and pleaded for forgiveness in their behalf.

4. Between certain circumstances and the person

Sometimes God reveals to us in advance bad things that are going to happen to someone. This can occur through a dream, a vision, a spiritual impression during a moment of prayer, etc. Obviously, if God is showing us something of this nature it is because He does not want it to happen. Intercessory prayer, in this sense, can make the difference between freedom and tragedy.

INCREASING THE POWER OF INTERCESSION

It would be beneficial to look at some of the catalysts that maximize the efficiency of the ministry of intercession. These elements are fundamental and need to be understood and exercised. Much of the spiritual battle orbits around these points.

1. The priestly perimeter of unity

Here we have the congregational call: *"if my people who are called by my name will humble themselves..." (2 Ch 7:14)*. It is essential to mobilize and unite people who carry the priestly mantle when dealing with territorial conquest and redemption. They must be called to humble themselves, pray, listen to God and consult with Him – this duty extends to all the people who live in the land (Jl 1:13-14). The more comprehensive this coverage, the greater the authority and the effects of the intercession.

2. Level of agreement

"Now I say to you that you are Peter (which means 'rock'), and upon this rock I will build my church, and all the powers of hell will not conquer it. And I will give you the keys of the Kingdom of Heaven. Whatever you forbid on earth will be forbidden in heaven, and whatever you permit on earth will be permitted in heaven" (Mt 16:18-19).

We have to address an important question: how do we deal with the gates and barriers of hell that hinder the establishment and edification of the church? We are not going to tear down the gates of hell with a lot of yelling. Jesus not only mentions the *"gates of hell,"* but also speaks of the *"keys of the kingdom of heaven."* A key is something that fits in a door. Clearly the understanding is that God does not see us as burglars but as locksmiths. We do not "sneak in;" we are sent with the keys that will bring salvation to the lost, reveal heavenly understanding, impart the spiritual gifts, gather the called, share the supernatural resources and free the captives. We carry the means to unlock the door to the cell where the prisoners are imprisoned. All we need are what Jesus calls *"the keys of the kingdom of heaven."*

But, what are these keys that unlock the resistance of Satan? Where does this power to open and close that which needs to be opened and closed come from? What was Jesus trying to say? Every door has a lock, even the gates of hell. The Bible says that these keys of death and hell were in Satan's power but were taken from him in Jesus' messianic conquest that culminated in his death and resurrection: *"I am the living one. I died, but look—I am alive forever and ever! And I hold the keys of death and the grave" (Re 1:18).*

This means that Satan no longer has possession of the keys of death and hell; they belong to Jesus! His victory was so complete that the devil even lost the keys to his house! Everyone he kidnapped, everything he stole and held captive in his territory can now be rescued. The work of the church is a search and rescue mission. However, opening a locked door is only a simple job and is only possible when you have the keys. When you do not have them, not only is the work cumbersome and risky, it is impossible!

Thus, the larger issue is no longer having to take these keys from the devil but receiving them from God! It is here that the unity Jesus prayed for comes to bear. He explains about the possession of the keys of the kingdom of heaven saying: Whatever you forbid on earth will be forbidden in heaven, and whatever you permit on earth will be permitted in heaven." He defines the meaning of these keys through a prayer of agreement.

The unity of the church establishes a connection between the physical and spiritual worlds, affecting the reality in both planes. The key that opens the gates of death is the church functioning through the practice of unity.

It is quite simple: the power to advance and edify the church against the demonic powers in any locality depends primarily on the level of agreement and the base of unity established by spiritual leaders, their ministries and their denominations. The problem is not the denominational "differences," but the denominational "divergences" – independence takes the place of interdependence.

I am not saying that we must have doctrinal unity but that we must simply agree with the diversity of the body of Christ and with the fact that we have a common enemy. Our struggle cannot be directed to a denominational competition; it must be directed against Satan and his hosts. The main strategy of every territorial principality is producing division and enmity between leaders and denominations. This is how the church loses the key that determines its ability to advance.

When pastors and leaders in a locality gather interdenominationally to pray, compassionately confessing their sins, the sins of the church, of government, of the city, etc., legitimately exercising their priesthood, an environment of agreement is established. This generational confession of sins, injustices and territorial corporate crimes through intercession unlocks the gates of hell. Hell is forced to give way to the Kingdom of heaven in the heart of the people and in the spiritual environment of their territory! This brings a great harvest. Any evangelistic effort will have a tremendous effect and produce tremendous results. All churches grow. We experience the bounty that God has for all of us!

3. The depth of spiritual brokenness and transparency of gathered intercessors, pastors and leaders meeting

This is another fundamental aspect of intercession. The flagship of restoration is humiliation. The more profound and genuine the collective brokenness, the greater the power of intercession.

4. The accuracy of spiritual mapping

The intelligence and the effectiveness of intercession reside in the accuracy of confessions that are made concerning iniquities that were committed and that enabled demonic oppression. The more precise the mapping of injustices and iniquities, the more effective will be the intercession. It is necessary to understand how Satan is demarcating the territory that is under his captivity and make smart confessions in order to bring God's presence back the to land.

5. Perseverance

The greater the perseverance, the more devastating is intercession's power against demonic strongholds. The greater the stability of the combination of communion, mapping, confession and intercession, the more instable these evil strongholds will become. The kingdom of God prevails!

BASIC PRINCIPLES IMPLICIT IN INTERCESSION

We want to look at some of the principles that are implicit in the practice of intercession. They are conceptually quite different from each other but for didactic clarity we are going to highlight each of them specifically in an attempt to understand them better.

1. The principle of justification

The main difference between prayer and intercession is that intercession has a redemptive facet. While prayer has power if done in the name of Jesus, intercession appeals not only to the name, but principally to the justifying power of the blood of Jesus. The sacrifice of Jesus was the most sublime act of intercession – He took our place on the cross. Each time we intercede for someone using the same principle, we set up the spiritual process of justification. The justification of a person and their lineage silences the accuser, deauthorizing their pernicious influences and persecution. In deliverance, "a pound of intercession has greater effect than a ton of prayer." An effective, consistent deliverance does not exist without intercession because the majority of burdens we carry are of a collective nature.

2. The principle of corporatism (right of identification)

Inspired by divine compassion, we can identify with the body to which we belong, be it familial, denominational, territorial, etc. This was the most relevant aspect of the sacrifice of Jesus. Becoming a man, he identified himself with the entire human race and assumed our conviction in order to fulfill our judgment. Jesus not only identified with our sins, pains and ailments but he also identified with God's own heart, offering forgiveness and access to the divine promises.

Through identification, not only can we feel what a person is feeling, but we can also pray the prayer of God's heart for him. It is in this that we experience, and carry others to experience, the power of divine compassion that releases the miracles and supernatural interventions into our lives.

3. The principle of rescue

When you intercede for someone by removing their blindness and intercessorially confessing their sins, you establish a process that is able to both rescue him from the situation and from the consequences that he and his offspring should suffer. Additionally, this creates a strong confrontation with malignant forces that are blinding, trapping and manipulating the person for whom we intercede. In this manner, we are not only ousting the demons but are enabling the action of God's presence in the person's favor. Thus, we bind the strongman and create an environment that offers the possibility of a release from captivity.

4. The principle of collision

Through intercession, we are not merely shielding a person but are colliding with demonically infiltrated forces and influences, in some cases placating them, but more often removing them. It is common for the intercessor to feel the impact of this collision during the deliverance process. It is possible for this collision to be so significant that there can even be the manifestation of symptoms in an intercessor because he had similar infiltrations in his life as did the person coming for deliverance. The result is that not only is the person receiving counseling freed from the demonic influence, but a person assisting in the ministering can receive the same liberation.

We must not, however, confuse collision with retaliation. A collision is a momentary collateral effect that the intercessor feels upon the impact of the power of the cross with the demons faced in a deliverance. Retaliation is when we are exposed to a counterattack and the enemy successfully takes advantage of existing gaps in our lives, relationships and spiritual armor, delivering a jarring blow to us. Do not be naïve; it does not work to simply utter a prayer prohibiting the enemy's retaliation. Prayer is not sufficient; you must close the opening.

5. The principle of the prophetic act

When you confess the sins of someone, you are creating a spiritual possibility for them to personally do the same thing. Intercessory confession activates the operation of the Holy Spirit over the person and convinces him of sin, righteousness and judgment. What occurs is that the intercessory process takes on a prophetic and creative nature.

An intercessory prophetic act is not a guessing or an attempt at predicting the future. It is an expression of faith and compassion that has the power to influence and shape the future reality.

It is important to understand that this methodology we are studying based on the model of deliverance counseling cannot be viewed as a closed and absolute mechanism which limits the action or intervention of God. It is essential to not restrict divine inspiration through any strategy or methodology, regardless of how functional it may be. In counseling there must always be enough space for prayer, creative intercession, prophetic acts, acts of identification and compassion, acts of justice and strategic reconciliations.

When we combine a methodology based on correct principles with the inspiration that releases the *"davá"* (the Hebrew word that means the creative action of God) we maximize the potential of our counseling. This balance is very present in the ministry of Jesus. Sometimes Jesus would confront the roots of the people's problems: the woman who was doubled over that needed an encounter with her traumatic past, the lepers who needed to have a encounter with their leaders, the paralytic that needed to forgive, etc. On other occasions he acted out of an inspiration based on faith, doing things very much out of the ordinary: anointing the eyes of a blind man with saliva, giving an order for Lazarus to come out of the tomb, cursing a fig tree, overturning the tables of the money changers, etc.

Indoctrination vs. Inspiration

Intercession used in the counseling process must be marked by creativity. Creativity is an indication of genuine and divine inspiration. We cannot simply follow a recipe or cookie cutter approach that worked with other counselees. Just because something worked with one person does not guarantee that it will work with another. Inspiration and God's guidance is the difference. If we are not careful in this sense, we can trap the person in a religious routine that will diminish the effectiveness of the counseling.

An important aspect of intercession is the prophetic act. The essence of a prophetic act lies in being obedient to specific direction given by the Holy Spirit. The prophetic act has no power in itself; its power is found in doing what the Holy Spirit leads you to do. Assigning power to a prophetic act is the active ingredient in animism. Animism assigns life, vitality or power to something that has none on its own. This is one of the primary foundations of spiritualist religions.

So you can understand what I want to convey I want to use an example. Would we have biblical support to say that if we anoint the door of our house with oil that God would protect our house? The answer is no. Does the oil that was consecrated to the Lord have some kind of power in itself? The answer is also no. Is it biblical to say that if we anoint a person with oil that he is blessed and protected regardless of the attitude of his heart towards God; again, no. There are people that we can pour out a bucketful of oil on their head and it will not make any difference if they are not willing to make changes in their life! It is useless to simply and mechanically anoint someone or something. To mystically believe in the power of these acts independent of specific direction given by God is to practice evangelical spiritism.

On the other hand, if you are ministering or praying for someone and the Holy Spirit guides you to anoint the person or his home and you obey, will the person or his home be protected? The answer is yes. Is there power in anointing oil? No. There is power in obedience; not in oil. We need to anoint who and what God is sending our way. The essence of God's manifestation lies in obedience and not in the mystification of an act or an element. The Bible assures us that God's blessings are within our reach if we obey His commandments and guidelines. In relation to prophetic acts, what we are saying about oil also applies to wine, a handful of dirt, stakes, or any other substance that we are guided to use. There are no rules about what we can or cannot use.

Something else that is essential in the understanding of prophetic acts: neither they nor the activity surrounding them are to be turned into doctrine. This castrates the power of the prophetic act; it ceases to be prophetic and becomes a form of religiosity devoid of power. Whenever we indoctrinate, whether with a prophetic act, a strategy, a ceremonial practice, an expression of God's move, a growth model, etc., we open a crack for the infiltration of a culture of religiosity. We begin to walk in the opposite direction of being guided by the Spirit.

Psychodramas – the power of creative intercession

Chapter 8 of Joshua relates the story of the overwhelming victory over Ai and reveals how a strategy directed by God can make all the difference in the process of deliverance and the conquest of the soul. We have already shown that Canaan is a typology of the soul that needs to be conquered. Ai literally means "heap of ruins." The city of Ai represents areas of our soul where we suffer great defeats, losses and disappointments. The initial defeat of Israel at Ai, reported in Chapter 7 of Joshua, shook the faith of the nation. Because of the curse of Achan, Israel suffered a heavy retaliation where 36 men were killed and the army was embarrassed.

Chapter 8 shows how this situation was reversed. The main theme of the chapter is how God used the fresh-on-their-mind defeat as a strategy for the great victory that was won. Reading the biblical account, we are given a bird's eye view of the scene that plays out: the Ai army is lured out from behind the protective walls of the fortress, leaving it completely unprotected. The army is led into an ambush, surrounded and totally destroyed.

Joshua, following God's strategy of attacking before dawn, positioned part of his army, thirty thousand men, hidden behind the city. At daybreak, Joshua and the other part of the army approaches the city provocatively as if to attack it. Thinking they will have another easy victory, the Ai army pours out of the city to attack them. Joshua feigns being defeated and retreats; his intent is to lure them further away from the city. The result is that all of the men of Ai enthusiastically pursue the Israelites sensing a second major victory at hand.

At the right moment, Joshua raises his sword, giving the signal for the attack of the now unprotected city to begin and it is totally destroyed and burned. When the Ai army sees the smoke rising from their fortress city, they become disoriented and disheartened, not knowing what to do and having nowhere to retreat to. Joshua and his army close the trap, now being joined with the other part of the army that sacked the city, annihilating the enemy. This battle becomes a massive victory and it was built on the ruins of the first defeat. Obedience to God's strategy made all the difference!

This is the perfect allegory of creative intercession through identification or what we also call a psychodrama. This is where the counselor identifies himself or another of his team as the one who caused the trauma for the person (whether a father, mother, teacher, etc.). In the role (identification) of the aggressor, he now humbles himself and asks for forgiveness. The "victim" is allowed to fully express himself and relives all the pain they had experienced at the hands of this aggressor. But this time the counselor interacts with the wound that was caused in a graceful and constructive way.

The brokenness of the counselor being identified as the offender does what the offender should have done. He acts in such a manner so that all the inner suffering, the shame and the pride of the person being ministered to are exposed, confronted, forgiven, crucified and eliminated. The experiences that come from these creative intercessions are powerful and often supernatural.

... I once was counseling a precious sister who had a family history marked by a profound existential loss. Her mother had become pregnant with her when she had an affair with a teacher. When he father learned of the pregnancy, fearing a scandal, he simply disappeared, leaving his job at the school and fled the city. Her mother did not have the courage to face what had happened and managed to hide the pregnancy from the family until the day she gave birth. It was a very painful and sad story.

As one of the primary reasons for her wanting counseling was the difficulty she had relating to her husband, I asked her how was her heart in relation to the father she had never known. She promptly said that everything was fine and that God had placed people in her path to replace that relationship. However, the Holy Spirit clearly told me that the opposite was true and that things had not been resolved.

Then, strategically, I understood that I should test her. I suggested that we pray together asking that God would create the opportunity for her to encounter her biological father so she could express to him all that she was telling me. We began to pray, and, suddenly, her soul erupted. In a flood of anger and pain, she began to verbally assault her father, saying that he was worthless and a coward, that he was not her father... She lost control of herself to the point that when she had calmed down she was both surprised and embarrassed at her reaction. It seemed that she did not know that those feelings had been repressed in her soul.

Then, crestfallen, sobbing, unexpectedly, something began to happen. God began to show her a scene. She began describing it aloud to me: "I'm seeing myself on top of a huge cliff... and I'm holding a wheelchair with a man seated in it." In a strange tone, she said: "...and this man is my father!" It seems that what I had suggested of God arranging a meeting with her father was happening faster than I had imagined and in a way that I never could have imagined. In a new wave of fury she said: "I'll throw him over the cliff!" Realizing what was happening in her heart, I intervened: "No! Don't do it! This is your chance to receive God's own heart through your father!"

God himself had prophetically placed her face to face with her prodigal father, luring out the "army of Ai" who inhabited the fortress of her soul. Then, spiritually representing her father, I started asking her forgiveness. It was the request for forgiveness that she would have never heard from her father. Insecurity, fear, anger, all began to breakdown. The city of Ai of her soul was in flames! She began to understand where God wanted to carry her with all this.

Her father needed her help more than she needed his. What he had done had made him an invalid. She now perceived the despair her father had experienced, the despair that had caused him to flee and the suffering that came as a result. The ambush was closed.

Finally, after coming down from the cliff helping her father, the vision ended. Her soul was free. This experience was a watershed in her life and in her relationships.

6. The principle of collectivity

Within a lineage, intercessory confession restores the places that were formerly plagued through the familial generations. As a result, when we Intercessorially confess the sins of our ancestors, we collide with the demonic forces and curses that have been housed for centuries in the lineage, creating a free spiritual environment over our family and offspring. We promote a collective benefit.

"Yes, Adam's one sin brings condemnation for everyone, but Christ's one act of righteousness brings a right relationship with God and new life for everyone" (Rm 5:18).

This text illustrates the intercessory aspect of Jesus' death that focuses on the power of intercession belonging to the body of Christ. It is this death sanctioned by corporate confession of sins and iniquities against our lineage that satisfies the justice of God. It removes the legal standing that we have granted to demons and reintegrates the right of the Holy Spirit to have influence over our family and descendants.

Curses are intrinsically collective. Their sinful influence, endorsed by multiple generations, can establish a type of collective memory or familial mental fortitude that handcuffs people to terrible misunderstandings based on sinful traditions that are expressed through idolatry, role reversal in marriage, immorality, alcoholism, etc. These situations become a pervasive pattern that pursues and can propagate for generations.

Just as one person's sin can have a consequence for many, by the same principle one person's intercession can redeem many from those same influences and consequences. Both sin and obedience have a collective and hereditary aspect. Just as sin leaves a legacy of curses, obedience leaves a legacy of divine promises for our offspring: *"...For the sin of this one man, Adam, brought death to many. But even greater is God's wonderful grace and his gift of forgiveness to many through this other man, Jesus Christ" (Rm 5:15).*

The law of inheritance also teaches that we do not inherit the guilt, but the consequences of sins not redeemed by our ancestors: *"When Adam sinned, sin entered the world. Adam's sin brought death, so death spread to everyone, for everyone sinned" (Rm 5:12).* We do not inherit Adam's guilt; we inherit the scathing consequence of his sin – death. It is impossible to inherit someone's sin or guilt because sin is a personal, moral and non-transferable choice. What we inherit are the physical, emotional and spiritual consequences of sin.

Obviously intercession deals only with the result and not the guilt of sin. This is an extremely important aspect of intercession that must be understood. When we confess the sins of another, that person's sins are not being redeemed from the blame or guilt of his sin. It does mean that the malignant influences and consequences produced through his action will be mitigated or cancelled over him and his descendants. Unfortunately, many sins leave irreversible consequences.

For this reason it is common, when one or more people of a family come together to recognize and confess their lineage's sins and iniquities, that relatives who were previously adamantly opposed to the gospel suddenly are touched by the revelation of the Spirit and become believers. This type of intercession is a powerful weapon to promote a family's salvation. The bandages and spiritual blockages, the mantle of curses and credit accumulated by generations of injustices are powerfully broken by intercession. The light of the Gospel of the glory of God bursts through the previous dense foliage of the heart.

DELIVERANCE IS NOT AN END IN ITSELF

Deliverance is part of what Paul calls "the whole counsel of God." Sanctification has multiple facets, and deliverance is only one of them. It is not everything. It is only the initial aspect of sanctification that eliminates the contamination that arose during our slavery in Egypt. It deals with all kinds of formal or informal servitude we arrange with demons. It widens the path to a life of increasing faith and obedience. However, whenever deliverance does not take the position of obedience, it becomes addictive and unhealthy. Deliverance that does not lead to obedience is always disastrous and becomes incomplete and dangerously reversible.

"We are human, but we don't wage war as humans do. We use God's mighty weapons, not worldly weapons, to knock down the strongholds of human reasoning and to destroy false arguments. We destroy every proud obstacle that keeps people from knowing God. We capture their rebellious thoughts and teach them to obey Christ. And after you have become fully obedient, we will punish everyone who remains disobedient" (2 Co 10:3-6).

The consummation of a victorious life only happens when it generates obedience in those areas of defeat that were transformed through deliverance. This is the pinnacle of spiritual warfare in our lives where we have consolidated the victory of the cross. Every attempt at deliverance that does not cause the person to reverse the cycle of disobedience fails the biblical directive of liberation theology. We cannot be naïve and reduce the process of liberation to a mere recital of long prayers of renunciation. The apex of God's purpose in deliverance is achieved through a posture of obedience!

DELIVERANCE IS FOLLOWED BY A PERIOD OF TESTING

This section complements the understanding of the previous. All deliverance is followed by a time of testing in those areas that were reclaimed through the deliverance process. It is not possible to maintain our new state of freedom without having to confront the old and be tested in those areas that we had experienced a history of failure. People who are tested and triumph are transformed.

We do not attain sanctity of character without spiritual testing. It is necessary to voluntarily exercise our choice of opting for the holiness of God. "Demonic retribution" is not simply a temptation or an expression of demonic rage against us, but is a divine test that aims to lead us to a stable and vigorous spiritual life.

It is possible to be attacked seven times stronger than we were accustomed. Jesus warned about the possibility of an evicted spirit returning with seven spirits worse than himself in a "shock and awe" counterattack to regain the lost territory. Resisting this shock test, because *the Spirit who lives in you is greater than the spirit who lives in the world*, the possibility of living in total freedom is one hundred percent.

Jesus also warned us that demons, when displaced, will seek rest in places that are convenient. Their preference is someone in our family who would give them space. The more likely scenario is that that will be circling our *"house"* (literally, "generation"), attempting to establish a strategic base for the counterattack.

It is interesting that many of us, when we become believers and experience a measure of freedom, encounter serious resistance and even outright hostility from family members. This is why Jesus said that our enemies would be our own family. What is happening is that we are being attacked by demons who previously had a hold in our life but are now coming at us through the people we most love. They, for some spiritual convenience, offered shelter to the enemy and he gained a strategic staging point for his counterattack.

This obviously is not an easy test. We need to discern the spiritual nature of the battle so that we do not fight on the battleground of the enemy's choosing. It is essential to have a bird's eye perspective so we do not engage flesh and blood enemies and that we fight "the good fight," not the bad one. Acting in the opposite spirit, i.e., not reacting with the spirit of offense that may be used against us by our family, we can begin to conquer our house for God. In this way, our deliverance begins to win a collective expression, becoming a springboard for a life of increasing holiness and authority.

5

THE CROSS OF CHRIST

The cross is the central point from which the principles of human redemption emanate. Any viable spiritual solution is in some manner connected to the essence of Christ's sacrifice:

- Sins need the pardon of the cross.
- Wounds need the restoration of the cross.
- Curses need the liberation of the cross.
- Sickness needs the healing of the cross.
- Irrational beliefs need the knowledge of the cross.

You can have an excellent diagnosis but if the remedy (treatment) is inadequate, there is no cure. Pastors, psychologists, psychiatrists, or any therapist who ignores the spiritual redemption mechanism established by the cross of Christ, more often than not, are doomed to frustration.

The cross is not the suffering or discomfort that others cause us, but it lies in our responsibility to deny ourselves in favor of a life reconciled with God's will. The essence of the cross is neither injustice nor difficulties that have been suffered in life, but above all, how we react internally to them. This is the main axis for the healing and development of the human soul.

The cross of Christ also represents the only viable means of rescue and redemption. It signifies all that God has provided to legally pay off our entire balance of injustices and sin that guarantee the demonic sanctions that imprison the human being.

Before the fall of man, Adam and Eve enjoyed four wonderful privileges:

- They enjoyed an intimate communion with the Creator and Father.

- They worked in full cooperation with Him.
- They had all of their prayers answered.
- They enjoyed the full protection of God.

However, after the fall, all of these privileges were lost. Besides sin causing them to lose these privileges of a life in paradise, they and their entire future lineage would be held hostage to four consequences:

- They become guilty of transgression against God.
- They died that same day, not physically, but spiritually.
- Their entire being became corruptible, weakened and tarnished.
- They become captives, subjugated by sin, by ego and, consequently, by Satan.

For salvation to be legitimate, it must meet all the needs of fallen man. Therefore, the plan of salvation that God has prepared in His infinite wisdom has the objective of meeting all the needs of our complex being.

The cross is the perfect plan of God, the only way God redeems man without failing to comply with His own law; through the cross, Jesus became the just and justifier of whoever believes in him. Only the cross establishes a salvation that is consistent with the law and the character of God. Paul says this is *"foolishness to those who are perishing, but to us who are being saved it is the power of God."* A wonderful paradox!

Currently, we have a kind of modern gospel that offers solutions for only the first two problems: guilt and spiritual death. In most cases, people are still in the same condition of perversion, more or less enslaved by sin and suffering the disciplinary measures of Satan. Salvation must blot out all these consequences and restore all of man's privileges that he lost.

THE THREE ASPECTS OF THE CROSS[1]

There is only one cross, but we cannot understand its full meaning at once. One of the great secrets of Paul is that he learned to put "Jesus crucified" at the center of his message and life. He preached

THE THREE ASPECTS OF THE CROSS

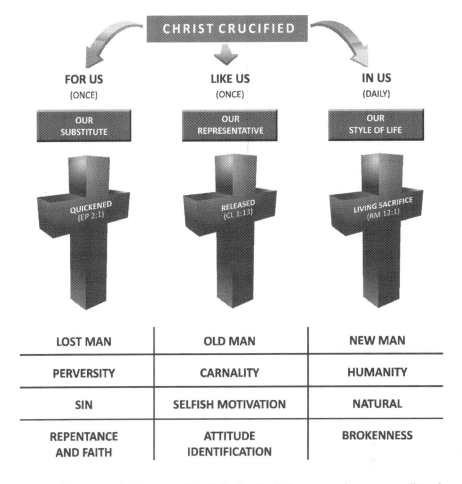

LOST MAN	OLD MAN	NEW MAN
PERVERSITY	CARNALITY	HUMANITY
SIN	SELFISH MOTIVATION	NATURAL
REPENTANCE AND FAITH	ATTITUDE IDENTIFICATION	BROKENNESS

Jesus Christ and him crucified (1 Co 2:2) because he was a "Paul crucified" (Gl 2:19). All references to the cross made in the Bible can be divided into three categories.

1. Jesus as our substitute

"He personally carried our sins in his body on the cross so that we can be dead to sin and live for what is right. By his wounds you are healed" (1 Pe 2:24).

---

[1] Three Aspects of the Cross is an approach developed by T. A. Hegre, founder of Bethany Mission, in his course "Victorious Life Seminar on the Cross of Christ."

This points to the fact that Jesus died in our place. Life for life, blood for blood, fulfilling the righteousness of God that says: "The one who sins is the one who will die." Jesus intercessorially assumed our condemnation, justifying our sins and also blessing us with every imaginable blessing in the heavenly realms. He gave up his position of the "one and only" of the Father; by his death and resurrection he became the firstborn among many brothers, incorporated the human race into the family of God, redeemed believers and made them heirs of a New Testament.

This first aspect of the cross relates to salvation's initial act and is concerned with the problem of guilt and spiritual death. The Bible clearly teaches that all men follow the example of Adam and fall into sin voluntarily, becoming guilty. God's commandment for us to be pardoned and justified in Christ is to repent and believe. It is the only possibility. It is impossible for someone to believe they can be saved if they do not repent. This is the functional logic of human consciousness. Repentance is not an arbitrary act that God has imposed but the obvious fact that we could not believe that we are forgiven unless we genuinely repent.

God has done His part: "...Christ died for our sins ... " (1 Co 15:3), "... he was pierced for our transgressions, he was crushed for our iniquities." (Is 53:5). Public justice was satisfactorily fulfilled. When Jesus gave his last breath on the cross, saying: "it is finished!" He simply did everything that was necessary so that any person could be saved and reacquire all lost privileges in Adam's fall.

To receive eternal life we must receive Christ as Lord and Savior. A supernatural "new birth" experience is implicit. However, shortly afterwards, we find that we have other needs besides forgiveness and the certainty of eternal life. There is something deeper in us that needs to be resolved. The second aspect of the cross relates to this attitude of sin, where we are hostages of our desires and uncontrolled feelings.

2. Jesus as our representative

"Those who belong to Christ Jesus have nailed the passions and desires of their sinful nature to his cross and crucified them there. Since we are living by the Spirit, let us follow the Spirit's leading in every part of our lives" (Gl 5:24-25).

Everything that happened to Jesus also needs to happen to us. We need to identify with Jesus, in his crucifixion, in his death, in his resurrection and glorification. Of course this is a process for each situation and area of our lives. Every motivation, desire or feeling that, by obedience, we crucify to death, identifying ourselves with the cross of Christ, will resurface in a glorified form. We experience the best of God. We seat ourselves in heavenly places with Him, in a position of authority and rest. We live a life of faith that generates greater faith and glory that carries us to higher levels of glory.

In this second aspect of the cross we deal with the issue of sinfulness. We can refer to it as the root of sin, the basic motive that inspires all the actions that we practice, the potential of our desires and feelings to be co-opted.

This is a deeper perspective of the cross. It was not just our sins—those acts that we practice — that Jesus bore on the cross; he also took us, the sin along with the sinner. He carried our sinfulness or the chronic tendency to please our ego and wildly satisfy our desires. This aspect of the cross teaches us to die, not to desire, but to what is improper or compulsive, that which enslaves us.

Sin is nothing more than an appeal to our emotions, desires and feelings to step over the limits established by God. To be more accurate, the concept of sin comes from an inner question. Who governs whom? Do we control our desires, feelings and emotions, or do they control us? It comes down to a matter of self-control. The source of power to exercise spiritual self-control that keeps us from sin resides in the lifestyle that Jesus demonstrated of denying ourselves. This is how we are touched by his grace. It is the great secret that leads us to enjoy a healthy soul and a vigorous spiritual life, full of achievements in the manner Paul declares: *"Sin is no longer your master, for you no longer live under the requirements of the law. Instead, you live under the freedom of God's grace" (Rm 6:14).*

We experience this second aspect of the cross when we decide to subjugate our desires and feelings to the control of the Holy Spirit. This is an essential meaning of the cross that ensures the quality of life and communion that we enjoy in Christ. Once forgiven, we now become free from the power of sin. It is when we purposefully resolve the conflict between walking in the flesh and living in the Spirit.

We would better understand all the experiences of the Christian life if we understood that it has two facets. These facets are actions but they also involve an acquisition of an attitude or a decision that is made as well as a style of life that accompanies this decision. Surrendering to God is a personal undertaking that needs to be continuously cultivated.

When a person does not find himself in the spiritual plan that he should be in it is because he does not know God's provision, he has not totally delivered himself to God or because he does not trust in God's power for some reason.

William Booth, founder of the Salvation Army, was often asked about the secret of his success. He always explained: "God has had all there was of me. There have been men with greater brains than I have, men with greater opportunities, but ... I made up my mind that God should have all of William Booth there was." When A. W. Tozer was asked "what does it mean to be crucified?" he replied: "People who are crucified with Christ have three distinct marks: first, they are facing only one direction; second, they can never turn back; and third, they no longer have plans of their own. "

These three aspects of Tozer's response help us to define the depth of our spiritual life, how to determine how deep the cross and God's power have penetrated into our soul. We can only have certainty that we have enjoyed this second aspect of the cross if we maintain:

• An irrevocable decision to not abandon our commitment and our hope in Jesus.
• An irrevocable decision to never surrender to spiritual achievements we have already made.
• A continuous attitude of surrender to the Holy Spirit, whenever He convinces us of anything.

We need to make this total surrender to God as a complete and unconditional surrender. The only word to define it is death; death to self, death to the principle of following our own path.

3. Jesus as our style of life

"He did not retaliate when he was insulted, nor threaten revenge when he suffered. He left his case in the hands of God, who always judges fairly" (1 Pe 2:23).

The third aspect of the cross is concerned with our crucifying Christ in us daily. The crucified Christ must have crucified followers. This has nothing to do with sin—because we learn to die to sin—but with the life that we will live from this point forward. The verse which best describes this life is this:

"And so, dear brothers and sisters, I plead with you to give your bodies to God because of all he has done for you. Let them be a living and holy sacrifice — the kind he will find acceptable. This is truly the way to worship him. Don't copy the behavior and customs of this world, but let God transform you into a new person by changing the way you think. Then you will learn to know God's will for you, which is good and pleasing and perfect" (Rm 12:1-2).

In Luke 9:23, Jesus affirms that we must take our cross daily and follow him. He establishes that there exists a daily living of this crucified life. This third aspect of the cross has various phases. The five characteristics that best describe this experience are: sacrifice, brokenness, discipline, intercession and a spirit of forgiveness. These values, when incorporated into our lifestyle and into our relationships, function as fertile soil for the blossoming of the most powerful revelations of God that are able to renew the mind and sharpen us with the good, perfect and pleasing will of God.

There is no use in trying to discipline the old man (the one we used to be). It is the new man that we need to discipline. God only has one destination for the old man: the cross and the tomb. We need to participate in the life giving power of the resurrected Christ.

Another way to describe the third aspect of the cross is through the *"spirit of the slain lamb."* We do not defend ourselves. We assimilate a proactive lifestyle, responding with tolerance, compassion and wisdom in the face of life's adversity and injustice. We understand the importance of reconciling resignation with willingness, serving God and our fellowman with a good heart.

This third aspect of the cross deepens in the same proportion that the revelation of God increases. It is a growth process that lasts our entire life. The more revelation we receive the more adjustments we make; so we travel the path of the righteous, a path that is like the aurora lights, growing in our intensity until that perfect day. The second aspect of the cross focuses on the "old man" while the third is aimed at the "new man."

The cross will continue to be applied to our life throughout our existence. The Holy Spirit alone does this, no one else. He will prune things that may not be sinful but that need to be removed so we can grow. He will apply the cross to our life, making it practical and personal for us.

THE CROSS AND DELIVERANCE MINISTRY

There is no freedom without the cross. Praying or shouting repeatedly that we are breaking a given curse in the name of Jesus simply does not work. Curses and demons are not going to stop their activity merely because we yell louder or whisper softer than them. We have no power over them because of the shrillness of our voice or by the insistence with which we repeat the same command. It simply does not work like that.

Everyone knows the story of the seven sons of Sceva who went around casting out demons *"in the name of Jesus whom Paul preaches" (At 19:13-17)*. The story suggests that they had no consistency in their ministry and no relationship with the cross (1 Co 2:2) that provided Paul's spiritual legitimacy. Instead of them expelling the demons, it was the demons that expelled them. They were beaten and publically embarrassed. This episode recounts one of the most powerful sermons preached in the Bible, oddly enough, by a demon: But one time when they tried it, the evil spirit replied, *"I know Jesus, and I know Paul, but who are you?" (At 19:15)*.

Every ministry that intends to operate in the field of spiritual warfare but is not centered on the cross of Christ becomes banal, unbalanced and ineffective. To deal with any type of demonic exploitation, it is necessary to have an intelligent interaction with the principles implicit in the blood of Jesus. In this sense, the blood of Jesus is the most appropriate weapon and should be used before the name of Jesus.

It is also useless to threaten or attempt to remove demons with phrase like "the blood of Jesus has power." We cannot use the blood of Jesus like a religious amulet. The power of the blood of Jesus depends on our relationship with the relevant principles of the cross of Christ. So, in deliverance, it is not wise to use the name of Jesus without using the blood. Not only might it be superficial, it might even be illegitimate. The power of the blood exerts its effects when triggered by an obedient and consistent attitude of being identified with the cross of Christ.

The deception of triumphalism[2] – magical prayers

The Gospel triumphalist relies on preaching and prayers that offer irresponsible solutions and benefits at the expense of biblical expectations. It wants those things that demand a price of obedience and perseverance to be free and immediate. It is a cheap gospel, a bonus that came at no cost. Triumphalism believes in a promise without commitment to the values inherent in the promise. It is a type of blind faith without fidelity and superstitious. This is the model of spiritual undiscipline, the anti-disciple and the flattered will.

We have already talked about this but I think it is important to reinforce the point. I do not want to take away the value of a prayer of faith or from the proper name of Jesus, the name that was established above all names. In the great majority of cases, deliverance involves a process that needs to be matched with brokenness, coherence and accountability. The true character of deliverance is sanctification; it is where we essentially deal with the impurities and trash of the soul. Deliverance without sanctification is a contradiction. It is here that the power of the cross comes into play. The Holy Spirit can only penetrate our lives to the same depth that the cross enters it.

Deliverance is not simply the result of a magical prayer that produces an easy solution. This is an illusion and only serves to nurture even more spiritual irresponsibility in accommodated people. It gives birth to evangelical hypochondria that transforms the church into a prison where many find themselves slaves to the prayer and deliverance lines.

Many have become slaves to "deliverance ministry," "prayer ministry" or any of its derivative nomenclatures. Every day the same demon is expelled. It ends up becoming a show in the church. You should not irresponsibly expel a person's demons without identifying them and treating the respective causes of their exploitation. In most cases this only produces stress. The demonized person must be

[2] Triumphalism is the attitude or belief that a particular doctrine, religion, culture, or social system is superior to and should triumph over all others.

adequately confronted about his persistent sins and the framework of passivity in his life that allows the demons an all-access pass.

Many go to a deliverance minister viewing him as a kind of "evangelical voodoo priest." Obviously the deliverance counselor is not a spiritual superman with spiritual super powers. He only helps people position themselves correctly with the Gospel, applying the right principles that produce the expected results.

Be careful with instant solutions. People want things quick and easy. This way of thinking of a gospel decentralized from the cross does not work in the spiritual kingdom. Few understand that paying the price is necessary to not fall into the mistake of a cheap grace. He who does not want to pay the price also places little value on spirituality.

We talk a lot about prospering and little about persevering; there is much discussion about receiving and very little about obeying. This creates people who are dependent and parasitic, predisposed to disillusionment. Illusion and disillusion are cause and effect. It is only a matter of time before impatience and selfishness are transformed into pure deception and bitterness. This is the grand dilemma of a life divorced from the responsibility of denying itself.

Another factor is that many who come out of the occult and the New Age movement have acquired a dangerous mindset. They are accustomed to selfishly manipulating and controlling people, situations, favors and profits. All that is necessary is to perform a ritual and everything comes running to fall at their feet. This is the shortcut that Satan proposed to Jesus after showing him the kingdoms of the world: *"I will give it all to you, if you will kneel down and worship me."*

The kingdom of God does not tolerate this type of ease and idleness of the soul. It is often necessary to resist, fight, force yourself, renounce, forgive, preserver, humble yourself, confess and even expose yourself. The cross carries a price; the biggest enemy that must be defeated is ourselves.

The danger of deliverance without blood

— The first error of deliverance "without blood," or without the cross, is to attack the symptoms of curses and neglect the search for causes. There is an exaggerated overemphasis on demons and diseases. We have already seen that it is impossible to consistently eliminate the symptoms without addressing their respective causes. It boils down to an endless cycle of breaking and expelling. These activities can even produce a momentary effect, but the spiritual situation will change little, if at all, and the true entry points will remain open.

Recently I was watching a child play with his pet cat. He was using a small flashlight to project a small ball on the wall and the cat was frantically trying to catch it. The cat with all his agility could not grab the "ball" because it was merely a projection, an abstract image. Many of us are trying to grab the point of light instead of turning off the flashlight. Deliverance deals with the flashlight and not with the projected image. Using the light (symptoms), we can find the flashlight (source causing the symptoms) and simply turn it off.

How should you not minister a deliverance session? Simply breaking, binding and expelling demons and curses in the name of Jesus. This would simply be an attempt to grab the beam of a flashlight. It is like giving an aspirin to treat a serious infection. The best you can hope for is a temporarily reduction in the patient's fever. It would not be long before the fever returned. The Bible is quite clear and simple: *"Like a fluttering sparrow or a darting swallow, an undeserved curse will not land on its intended victim"* (Pr 26:2).

Curses and demons never take up residence without a "landing zone." There is always a reason. Focusing on expelling demons is like shooing away crows. It is momentary. They fly away and, after wandering a bit, return to land again in the same place. This is a "shoo" ministry that boils down to chasing out demons each time they return. A genuine deliverance involves destroying the landing zone. The demons do not return because they have lost their place.

— Another error of a bloodless deliverance lies in focusing in "revelation" only, ignoring the necessity of revealing and crucifying the causes of a curse.

I remember the ministry of a pastor who divined where works of witchcraft, amulets and other such paraphernalia were hidden. He had startling revelations about deliverance and prayed for people, leaving them quite impressed. However, he never spoke of repentance, confession of sins, restitution, holiness, etc. His greatest tonic was his accommodation. It is difficult to evaluate the true motivation of people, but it came to light that the moral life of the pastor was seriously compromised and he had been involved in several cases of adultery.

A group of his ministers conducted spiritual warfare vigils on a mountain where they corporally fought with demons. There was no attempt to teach or utilize the armor of the cross. This type of "spiritual battle" had more in common with the occult than with Christianity. There did not appear to be much difference between this pastor and his teachings and that of a voodoo priest and his teachings in the occult. He and his followers were having illicit access to the spiritual world governed by demons, conducting "spiritual warfare" inspired by occultic gifts that were received hereditarily or through alliances realized prior to salvation or even through the laying on of this pastor's unclean hands.

Unfortunately, these ministers, as well as the people they ministered to, ended up seriously involved in spiritual confusions and disturbances. Many became disillusioned and ended up leaving the church in a situation even worse than when they had entered.

We live in a time of much mysticism and sorcery. Many of these people when converted already called themselves leaders, pastors, and missionaries and wanted to minister to people. Since they were not yet sufficiently purified, when they laid their hands on and ministered to people, they transferred their impurities and caused more problems than gave solutions.

Conclusion

All demonic authority relies on human transgression of God's commandments. When we serve in a ministry of deliverance, we do not just understand the destructive power of sin but we also learn to abhor it, avoid it and personally and intercessorially confess it. Real deliverance is always inspired by the fear of God that glorifies the cross of Christ.

> "The message of the cross is foolish to those who are headed for destruction! But we who are being saved know it is the very power of God" (1 Co 1:18).

6

THE PROCESS OF EVALUATION

After crucifying the supposed causes of curses that were diagnosed in the deliverance process, we need to evaluate the results that were obtained in relation to the initially presented symptoms.

Evaluation is the process of comparing and confirming symptoms presented before and after a deliverance in order to improve the results. A deliverance can only be considered successful when the initial symptoms that validated the curses are eliminated or drastically improved. This is an important aspect that is needed to ensure the sustainability of the freedom that was won.

If the initial symptoms have remained unchanged, there was probably an error in the mapping process, the process of crucifying the causes or in both. It is necessary to continue excavating these areas until the deliverance process has been fully completed. Poor results may involve different situations that need to be addressed and raises an intriguing question: why are some people not freed? In this chapter I want to explore some of the common factors that are possibly preventing a person from being set free.

WHY ARE SOME PEOPLE NOT SET FREE?

1. A lack of the truth: open lies and hidden truths

The most basic principle for successful deliverance is exposing the whole truth: *"you shall know the truth, and the truth shall make you free" (Jn 8:32)*. Any distortion, withholding or concealing of the truth undermines the entire process. It is assumed that when a person seeks to be free he is willing to be bound to the truth, but in practice it is not what always happens.

There are people who will lie when in a deliverance session and others who will dodge fundamental truths. Obviously in both these situations the person fails to overcome the shame he feels and chooses to stay on the defensive in relation to his reputation. Behind every lie there are rigid structures of pride that harbor and support a chronic state of spiritual persecution and imprisonment.

Spiritual freedom is fully conditioned on our loyalty to the truth: *"if we confess our sins to him, he is faithful and just to forgive us our sins and to cleanse us from all wickedness" (1 Jn 1:9).* Normally, when a person seeks spiritual freedom there always exists a sinful situation that must be exposed and dealt with. The more difficult a sin is to confess, the stronger it imposes its spiritual imprisonment. These mental resistances function as internal bases of support that serve to malignantly exploit a person's life.

God does not require us to confess every sin we have ever committed in our life. That would be like bursting open a feather pillow and picking up each one of them. However, it is often the case that a particular sin or abuse has served as the door that has opened us up to significant loss or failure in our lives. Until this is acknowledged and confessed, the whole process comes to a standstill.

A person can go through scores of deliverances with the best counselors and intercessors; however, as long as he is not exposing the whole truth that needs to be revealed he will never be free.

2. Lack of repentance

Proverbs 28:13 expresses an infallible law: *"People who conceal their sins will not prosper, but if they confess and turn from them, they will receive mercy."* After confession, repentance is the next fundamental step, i.e., after we have confessed our sin we need to leave it. When we take the position of firmly resolving to stop the practice of the sin, we are immediately touched by God's mercy.

Many want to get rid of the uncomfortable consequences of demonic oppression; but this is not sufficient reason to be free of it. We cannot enjoy genuine spiritual freedom without abandoning the practices that sustain the curse. God's blessings are directly linked to His commandments.

If the person is not disposed to mold himself into God's character, suffering the necessary changes that need to take place, his spiritual freedom will not be sustainable. Every victory temporarily won in deliverance will simply fall apart, and can even make the situation worse than it was, if true repentance is not practiced.

3. Lack of reaction – spiritual slothfulness

This is one of the most important principles of spiritual warfare: *"If you fail under pressure, your strength is too small" (Pr 24:10)*. The deliverance process demands emotional force, energy (moxie) and moral fiber. There are times when we have to fully rise to the occasion and use all of our energy if we want to overcome our "day of distress."

If we want freedom, we must understand the real situation we are in. A cruel enemy who wants to relentlessly destroy us binds us. It is vital that we react; understanding the sufficiency of Jesus' sacrifice and the immense advantage it gives us. Sadly, not every person who submits to spiritual discipleship understands that deliverance is a struggle and that the fight may be temporarily intense.

The person who takes a slothful and passive posture, besides compromising the results of deliverance, literally places his head on a platter and willingly hands it to his enemy, allowing him to fully control the situation. It is worth mentioning here the two primary reasons why someone's deliverance process will be prolonged much longer than is necessary and be characterized by demonic manifestations that should not happen in the believer's life:

— ***Doors of carnality***. The person is living in hidden, and even compulsive, sin. This practice transforms the deliverance process into a long and exhausting exercise where demons are exiting and returning to the person, making for a stressful process. These sessions can be extremely painful for the person.

If there is no discernment as to what is occurring and there is never a specific confrontation of the person and his sin, the attempt at deliverance becomes a dead end where demons become the show. It is common to see inexperienced liberators going on for hours, even days/weeks, trying to deal with this type of situation. There are almost never any beneficial results.

— *Doors of passivity*. The person does not react. He has a weak will, is subservient to feelings and his mind is susceptible to intimidation and self-condemnation. He never assumes his rightful position in Christ. Typically this is additionally reinforced by a weak and superficial relationship with God.

Few churches today place emphasis on a daily devotional life based on relationship with God's Word and prayer. A secret life of relationship with Abba is the great secret of a spiritual life. Most church models produce a spiritually dependent following, whether it is a dependency on leaders, meetings, programs, etc. This is an error in the infrastructure of many ministerial visions and theological seminaries. It is the reason so many people accommodate a passive spiritual life that is dependent, irrelevant, selfish and even mundane.

We live in an era of diversion and self-absorption. Ours is a culture of comfort and hedonism. Many religions and popular therapies have taught people to "turn on, tune in, drop out".[1] Many psychiatrists avoid the problems brought to them; it is simply more convenient to prescribe a drug that only momentarily relieves the undesirable side effects of the problem, but without affecting its roots. The axis for the healing of the soul resides in the power of rationing, in the initiative to change what needs to be changed and to be changed by the grace of God. It is vital to react purposefully, making the necessary adjustments to lifestyle.

People who become involved with the numerous techniques, religions, sciences and exercises of the New Age movement have a strong tendency toward spiritual indolence. Because of that spiritual passivity there is a need of an increased piety to fortify their will.

The more vulnerable we are, the more the power of God has an incredible ability to perfect us in our weakness. We cannot allow intimidation to enter. It is necessary to react, resist, position, and clamor. When our will aligns with the will of God we experience the supernatural power of liberating faith. Otherwise, we remain in a state of captivity.

---

[1] "Turn on, tune in, drop out" is a counterculture phrase popularized by Timothy Leary in 1967.

4. Wrong or futile motives

God is pleased when we turn to Him seeking his help and restoration; but if there is something He takes into account, it is our motivations. James makes this quite clear: *"even when you ask, you don't get it because your motives are all wrong—you want only what will give you pleasure" (Ja 4:3).* Typically, our greatest problem is not the lack of deliverance but exactly these futile motivations that have been diverted from the divine purpose.

Despite our suffering and spiritual discomfort, God will not stop profoundly treating that which needs to be treated. God is not afraid of saying "NO!" He is not afraid of how we are going to react when He opposes our corrupt motives and does not answer our torturous prayers. He is not manipulated by our spiritual tantrums and will never endorse our stubborn, bitter, rebellious and wicked motives.

God offers freedom to those who are going to promote His purpose; not for those who want to continue in a comfortable, selfish, futile life that has no eternal significance. Our motivations need to be tuned to the values of the Gospel. When there are corrupted or strange intentions regarding the Spirit of God, the person's deliverance and freedom are compromised.

5. Self-centered people – the lust for attention

Some people always feel ignored and non-important. They want to be in the center but life in some form or the other always pushes them to the sidelines. They feel that no one cares about them. One possible reason is that they are oppressed and suppressed by demons. Basically, this chronic desire for attention is idolatry in relation to an emotional deficit, a cult of suffered rejection or a church of "woe is me." Sadly, this self-pity destroys the power of deliverance.

When these people seek spiritual counseling in deliverance, they suddenly perceive that they are the center of attention and they like it. When they receive some measure of freedom through the deliverance process, they regress because they think that the people who were helping them are no longer giving them the same attention they were giving in the beginning.

6 | THE PROCESS OF EVALUATION

PART II - ANALYSING THE DIAGRAM

INTELLIGENT SHEPHERDING

They begin to prolong the problem as if there is something else that needs to be treated; the truth is that they do not want freedom, they want attention! When the deliverance counselor no longer gives them the attention they desire, they look for someone else. This symptom of the lust of acceptance may be diagnosed when the deliverance process begins to be drawn out indefinitely. Any counseling requires a beginning and an end; there comes a time when the person must be capable of responsibly walking on their own two feet.

The objective of the counselor is to leverage the person's emotional dependence to a position of interdependence. The counselor can never allow the counselee to transfer his responsibilities to him. This is the great risk of codependency. The immature counselor feels valued by this chronic attitude of dependency from the counselee, while the counselee feels loved by the condescending counselor. Instead of making a disciple, the person ends up creating a parasite.

This impoverished and manipulative spirit needs to be crucified; otherwise, the person remains susceptible to demonic exploitation. The co-dependency can cause counseling to be prolonged indefinitely without ever bringing any real benefit. This can occur in discipling, pastoral counseling or in psychological and psychiatric counseling; this is a real danger in any counseling setting where the emphasis is on the dependency on the therapist, the therapy, the medication, etc.

We also need to be on the alert that devouring the precious time of counselors is one of the principle strategies of the enemy. We need to be especially attentive to this tactic. As Paul says of such people: *"[they] are forever following new teachings, but they are never able to understand the truth" (2 Tm 3:7)*. The highest principle needed to produce maturity is emancipation. One of the best ways to help someone in counseling is to not tolerate dependency; establish the investment in the emotional, moral and spiritual emancipation of the person as the essential purpose of the counseling.

6. Failure to break with the occult

While it seems simple in theory, in practice it is very difficult for someone involved in the occult to break off involvement completely. We live in a time where there is a revival in witchcraft, sorcery and vampirism. The stories of people involved in the occult are increasingly astonishing. Satan knows how to create a series of situations that will spiritually anchor a person's life in subservience to him. Many compromising involvements within the occult are orchestrated, then the memory stolen by the very enemy who fostered the situation, trapping the person in ways they cannot remember. Many pacts and incriminating entanglements happen without the person even being aware of it or while in a trance or during moments of demonization while participating in occult activities. In some cases the process demands a supernatural intervention of God.

As already mentioned, the occult also addicts the person to power. Many are subtly enchanted by the supernatural and end up opening a crack for the enemy to enter and act. The fascination with spirituality can easily sustain demonic exploitation in someone's life and compromise his ability to break free.

7. Failure to break manipulative and selfish relationships

This is very common when strong soul ties have been created through illicit sexual or perverted relationships. Many of these relationships involving dating with fornication, homosexuality, lesbianism, etc., essentially become unhealthy and represent an intense focal point of demonic exploitation. The principle characteristic of an unhealthy relationship in this sense is an emotional dependency where the person remains vulnerable to continuing in an abusive or immoral relationship.

Sometimes it is not easy for a person to break free of selfish pressure or from someone who wants to manipulate him. Even though some relationships are outrageously abusive, the person will conform to the situation and stay in it. In others, the person will actually begin to develop false guilt when they try to establish limits in a relationship with a jealous boyfriend, a violent spouse, a controlling leader, a possessive friend or a dependent mother (widow or divorcee) that feels threatened when an adult child decides to marry or otherwise get on with their lives.

It does not matter how close these relationships are; the person's liberation will not occur until he breaks free of the control and manipulation that the person is exerting over his life. Firmness and wisdom will be necessary. The adjustment process in these relationships will certainly not be easy, but this will be essential to gaining total freedom and deliverance.

Sometimes a courageous conversation will be necessary, frank and directly addressing these structures of insecurity, rejection and traumas. It must establish the respect and individual space that has been stifled.

In other cases it will be necessary for the person to break off the relationship entirely, remove himself completely from the other person's life and allow God to reestablish the relationship in His time and on His terms.

8. Failure to completely break away from the curse

Addressing a curse involves good spiritual discernment of our history and our activities. It also involves a lifestyle of intercession, especially in regards to our families, ministerial coverage and church involvement that continue in a sinful state. There are several common indicators that alert us to the existence of a curse over someone. If you recognize these oppressive forces influencing you in an abnormal manner, recognize it as a call to intercession.

There may also be important information that dictates a genuine need for intercession and this information may still need to be discovered and crucified. Many cases of personal deliverance are directly connected to family history. Observant attention is necessary to evaluate persistent curse symptoms, taking care to map episodes of injustice and corresponding repetitive inequities that are uncovered in the family tree. This can be a fairly lengthy process. However, if we persevere in the exercise of this kind of priesthood, it will only be a matter of time until we experience a break in the spiritual realms over our lives and the lives of our family.

9. When the problem is of a natural or organic origin

Not every psychoemotional disorder is spiritual. In some cases it is very important to direct a person to a physician or specialist. This does not deny that psychosomatic symptoms can be anchored in a spiritual disorder; but there are some situations where the problem is totally physiological and if the person does not receive the appropriate help, they will never be free of the symptoms.

Of course God can heal any type of disease or organic disorder and it is for this reason that we are to always pray for this intervention.

10. When it is not a question of deliverance but of reeducation

Many, especially those who are already prepared to go through deliverance, may be waiting for certain changes to take place in their lives that are not tied to their deliverance but to the vital need for re-education. Deliverance that is not accompanied by re-education (rehabilitation) can produce a dangerous setback where the person ends up worse than before.

Deliverance releases the person but does not restore that which was atrophied. This requires re-education at the level of the identity, sexuality, character, will, financial management, etc. In the same manner that someone who has been bedridden for months has muscles that atrophy and must go through rehab to restore them, so it is in the spiritual realms regarding our spiritual "muscles." It is unfortunate that many simply assume that the deliverance process granted them the restoration of their soul in a couple of hours and attempt to resume their life as though everything has been "fixed." A person who has been corrupted by a demon that caused him to spend wildly will not know how to practice financial management unless he is taught now that he can properly process the teaching. Just because the demon left does not now mean the person knows how to take care of his money; dangerous habits are still in place.

This incorrect perspective is highly frustrating. It is necessary to understand that for the whole process of deliverance to be maintained, it is necessary to couple it with a process of re-education. This is what will infallibly produce character and sustainability.

Printed in the United States
By Bookmasters